WHAT PEC
FOR (
CONSIDERING THE CALL TO MILITARY CHAPLAINCY

"Brian Bohlman's book is an essential resource for those seeking fresh theological perspectives and vocational discernment regarding the ministry of a Military Chaplain. Written with the passion of a pastor who answered God's call to take the Gospel to members of the Armed Services, this study will be valued by anyone seeking clarity on a decision to enter the Military Chaplaincy. Professional clergy, seminary students, and congregations must read and reflect upon the research of this superb book."

DOUGLAS L. CARVER, Chaplain (Major General) USA (Ret.)
Executive Director of Chaplaincy, N. American Mission Board
22nd Chief of Chaplains (2007-2011), United States Army

"The dissertation and research that resulted in this book fills a big gap in current literature about discerning the call to ministry as a Military Chaplain. The expansive list of over 325 unique Chaplaincy ministry websites will be a one-stop resource for those desiring to serve in any of the major functional areas of Chaplaincy. I highly recommend this book to anyone who aspires to serve as a Chaplain."

MICHAEL W. LANGSTON, CAPT, CHC, USN, (Ret.)
Professor of Chaplaincy
Seminary and School of Ministry
Columbia International University

"Brian's doctoral dissertation which resulted in this book is based on the highest quality of scholarship. His research on why persons answer the call to Chaplain ministry remains ground-breaking and established him as a leading authority on this topic and related questions. Just as I routinely use his dissertation as an example for other students to emulate, I give this book my highest recommendation for any current or future Chaplain in the U.S. Armed Forces."

R.J. GORE Jr., D.Min., Ph.D.
CH (COL) U.S. Army Reserve (Ret.)
Dean of the Seminary and Professor of Systematic Theology
Erskine Theological Seminary

"Chaplain Bohlman has undertaken an important study of the nature of call not only to ordained ministry in general, but to the specific and specialized ministry of Chaplaincy in the Armed Forces of the USA. He not only believes that the vocation of Military Chaplaincy is a high and honorable calling from God (an act of ministry that involves an initial call from God, the confirmation of the Church, and the obedience of the person), he also demonstrates the validity of the call through Biblical insights (lifestyle ministry, presence, shepherd, servant hood, pastoral care, etc.), careful exegesis of the text, and a study of persons who are discerning their own call to ordained ministry and Chaplaincy. I expect this study to be of great value to men and women of any denomination who are pondering the concept of their call to serve both God and Country as Chaplains in the military services."

ROBERT G. CERTAIN, Ch, Col, USAF (Ret.)
Executive Director
Military Chaplains Association of the USA

"Every year thousands of men and women respond positively to a sense of "call" and matriculate to graduate schools of theology and seminaries of many faiths to discover the area of ministry they are specifically called to. Some of them will answer the call to serve outside the walls of a traditional place of worship as a Chaplain. This book will greatly aid those considering the call in any of the functional areas of Chaplaincy to reflect both personally and theologically on performing or providing pastoral and spiritual care to all persons as a professional Chaplain. I heartily welcome and commend this book as an excellent, practical resource for ecclesiastical endorsers to provide to any person seeking to become an endorsed Chaplain."

DAVID B. PLUMMER, BCC, LMFT
Director, Sentara CarePlex Hospital Chaplaincy Services
Endorsing Executive, Coalition of Spirit-Filled Churches
Former Chair of the COMISS Network and
Endorsers Conference for Veteran Affairs Chaplaincy

For God and Country
Considering the Call to Military Chaplaincy
(Revised Edition)

Brian L. Bohlman

Chaplain Resource Center
West Columbia, SC

For God and Country:
Considering the Call to Military Chaplaincy (Revised Edition)
Copyright © 2015 Brian L. Bohlman. All rights reserved.

ISBN 13: 978-1507602133
ISBN 10: 1507602138
Amazon.com/Author/BrianBohlman

Published by Chaplain Resource Center
PO Box 5235, West Columbia, SC 29171
ChaplainResourceCenter.com

Note: This revised and updated edition contains a new and updated appendix with a vast list of resources in the major functional areas of Chaplaincy. The approved Erskine Seminary 2008 Doctor of Ministry Chaplaincy project dissertation is also included from the first edition.

This book or parts thereof may not be reproduced in any form, stored in a retrieval system, or transmitted by any means--electronic, mechanical, photocopy, recording, or otherwise--without prior written permission of the author, except as provided by United States copyright law.

Unless otherwise noted, Scripture references are taken from the Holy Bible: New International Version. Copyright 1973, 1978, 1984 by International Bible Society. Used by permission of Zondervan Publishing House. All rights reserved.

Cover design by JoleeneNaylor.com. Cover photo courtesy of DoD. Used with permission. Use of cover photo does not imply any type of endorsement. The views expressed or implied in this book are not necessarily the official views of, or endorsed by, the U.S. Govt. or any service branch in the Department of Defense.

Other books by Brian Bohlman available at:
Amazon.com/Author/BrianBohlman
So Help Me God: A Reflection on the Military Oath (E-book or Print)
ISBN 13: 9780976681908
ISBN 10: 0976681900
NSN: 9925-01-547-9476

ACKNOWLEDGEMENTS & DEDICATION

First and foremost, I want to thank God for the opportunity to complete a Doctor of Ministry degree. The writing of a dissertation often demands much time and attention away from one's family. Therefore, the following persons must be acknowledged for their ongoing support in this academic undertaking:

My wife, Shelley, for her patience and sacrifices made over the years. My daughter, Mary Ellen, for her prayers and encouragement. My mother, Vicky, for her keen eye and editorial assistance. The staff and faculty of Erskine Theological Seminary, especially Drs. R.J. Gore, Richard Burnett, Loyd Melton, and James Hering for their wisdom, guidance, and instruction. Thank you for your dedication and devotion to working with military Chaplains over the years.

The staff and faculty of Columbia International University, especially Drs. Robertson McQuilkin, George Murray, Bill Jones, Don Hamilton, Roy King, and Rick Higgins who offered their support and encouragement to conduct this project with seminary students. I am honored that Dr. John Harvey and Dr. Michael Langston fulfilled the vision and established a robust and Chaplaincy program at CIU in 2011.

Thanks to the seminary students at Columbia International University and Liberty University who offered their time to participate in the Consider the Call Prospective Military Chaplain Workshop. Without you, this book and project would not have been possible.

My journey into the military Chaplaincy spanned over a ten-year period as the Lord used a vast array of people to help me discern my call to ministry in the U.S. Armed Forces. Therefore, this Chaplaincy book, project and dissertation are dedicated to those who encouraged me to consider the call to military Chaplaincy as well as those who will answer the call to military Chaplaincy in the future. My prayer is that God would use the words on these pages to help others who are considering the military Chaplaincy as a vocation.

CONTENTS

Acknowledgments and Dedication — v

Introduction to Revised Edition — viii

Foreword — ix

Chapters

1. Military Chaplain Recruiting as an Act of Ministry — 1
2. Chaplain Literature Review — 19
3. Biblical Insights into the Call to Military Chaplaincy — 33
4. Designing a Consider the Call Chaplain Workshop — 57
5. Results and Evaluation of the Workshop — 73

Appendix

A. Prospective Military Chaplain Survey (Blank) — 97
B. Prospective Military Chaplain Survey (Results) — 103
C. Session One Workshop Questionnaire — 111
D. Session Two Workshop Questionnaire — 113
E. Session Three Workshop Questionnaire — 115
F. Workshop Evaluation Survey (Blank) — 117
G. Workshop Evaluation Survey (Results) — 120
H. Workshop Participation Record — 123
I. Chaplaincy Resource List — 124

Notes, Bibliography, and Other Sources Consulted — 182

About the Author — 200

LIST OF TABLES

Table

1. Service Locations of CIU Alumni
2. CIU Statistics of Seminary/Grad School Alumni/Enrolled
3. CIU Graduating Student's Vocational Location Goals
4. CIU Graduating Student's Vocational Organization Goals
5. Spiritual Gifts and Abilities of Prospective Military Chaplains
6. Non-Ministry Occupational Experiences of Prospective Military Chaplains
7. Undergraduate Degree Concentrations of Prospective Military Chaplains
8. Motivational Factors that Influenced Decision to Become a Military Chaplain
9. Persons Rated Most Influential in Decision to Become to Military Chaplain
10. Prior Military Service as an Influential Factor to Become a Military Chaplain
11. Desired Military Service Branch and Duty Status as an Influential Factor to Become a Military Chaplain
12. Military Chaplain Candidate Program as an Influential Factor to Become a Military Chaplain

INTRODUCTION TO REVISED EDITION

Since the original e-book edition of this book was first released in 2011, I have been humbled to learn how God has used this book to help persons discern their call to serve in the Military Chaplaincy. Over the last several years, many readers have encouraged me to expand the original edition by providing additional resources to take the next step in answering the call to Military Chaplaincy.

This new and revised edition, which is now available in paperback for the first time, is in direct response to those requests. With the rapid growth of professional Chaplaincy into many other non-military Chaplaincy settings, readers will enjoy over 55 pages in a new appendix which includes a plethora of resources for Military Chaplaincy as well as nine other major functional areas and subareas of professional Chaplaincy.

With the rise of many graduate schools of theology and seminaries offering degree programs with a Chaplaincy concentration, I added an entire new section to help prospective students ponder some very important questions when choosing a place of study. Another new section in the appendix includes website links to many Chaplaincy and Chaplaincy related organizations and associations. This section will be a helpful desk reference and resource for anyone exploring the vast array of Chaplaincy settings in North America and around the world.

Finally, it is my hope and prayer that God will continue to guide those who are prayerfully considering serving as a professional Chaplain outside the four walls of a traditional place of worship. Many Chaplains have entered this specialized field of ministry because someone took the time to listen and help them discern God's call on their life. In like manner, I would encourage you to give a copy of this book to anyone who is contemplating the call to ministry as a Chaplain. Thank you.

Brian Bohlman
January 2015

FOREWORD

This book is an essential resource for any individual who is sensing a call into the service of Military Chaplaincy. It is clear and concise in its guidance and clarifies the steps to truly discern the calling of God into not only the military, but also the high calling of being a spiritual reference and resource to today's military men and women. As the real world operational challenges on our service members and their families become greater and greater, it is the Chaplain who will often help the Soldier, Sailor, Airman or Marine to have the moral and physical courage to face the rigorous demands of military life in a time of war.

The role of Military Chaplain is a very demanding one, and not for everyone. Deployments and long separations from families, the dangers of serving in hostile areas, often alongside combat soldiers, and the demands of military officer career development quickly separate the wheat from the chaff among possible candidates to this esteemed corps. Dr. Bohlman lays out precisely the concerns and questions any person should have when seriously considering this unique field of ministry.

As a former Commander of troops and counselor to young Soldiers and junior officers, I wish I would have had such a wonderful tool in my arsenal to help guide the men and women who desired to explore this profession. I can and do highly recommend this work to any person, in uniform or not, who has ever considered joining the elite ranks of our professional Chaplain Corps.

RICHARD R. CURREN III
Captain, United States Army (1986-2002)
Creator and Producer of Scaly Adventures TV Show
Co-Founder of Boundless Limits International
Author of *On Course: Strategies For Successful Living*

CHAPTER 1

MILITARY CHAPLAIN RECRUITING AS AN ACT OF MINISTRY

The Call to Military Chaplaincy

Since the earliest days of the American colonial period, members of the clergy have answered the call to serve their God and Country as military chaplains. Dr. John Brinsfield, senior historian for the U.S. Army Chaplain Corps, documents the origins of the American military chaplaincy. In discussing the historical background of the birth of the military chaplaincy, Brinsfield has said the following:

> The chaplain, clad in his suit of black broadcloth, *accompanied the colonial militia* into battle from the very beginning. The colonial forces were locally recruited and when they went to war they *took with them one of the local ministers*, who usually, but not always, was one of the younger and more physically able of the clergy. It was an age when religion played a much more important role in the lives of Americans. For the colonist, the minister was a powerful figure of authority within the community. Not even a minor military operation was planned or carried out without making sure that *a minister was available* to counsel and motivate the colonial fighting man. The Reverend Samuel Stone of the Church of Christ in Hartford, Connecticut, is an example of the power and authority exercised by the chaplain.

Military Chaplain Recruiting as an Act of Ministry

The Reverend Stone was the *first military chaplain* to begin his active field service in English America. Earlier chaplains accompanied expeditions to the New World. Stone served in the Pequot War of 1637, the first large scale Indian conflict in New England.[1]

In the 1770s, during the American Revolution, General George Washington formalized the military chaplaincy. From the Revolutionary War to the present War on Terror, thousands of clergy members have answered the call to tend to the souls of warriors during times of peace, state and national emergencies, natural disasters, and war.

In doing so, American military chaplains have become heroes of faith and freedom. According to retired Army Chaplain, Brigadier General Wayne Hoffman, past president of the Military Chaplains Association, "Chaplaincy is a unique vocation—it is a call within a calling. Distinctive as it is, balancing one's call from 'God' with one's call to serve our nation is a distinction that is shaped more clearly by understanding the multi-dimensional shape of the military chaplaincy."[2] Therefore, the role of the military chaplain has always had unique challenges. Historian Stephen Mansfield discusses some of the issues that confront military chaplains in today's world. According to Mansfield,

> America's military chaplains occupy what must surely be among the most unique [sic] positions in the world. Theirs is a universe of contradictions. They are a holdover from an earlier age of faith, much like congressional chaplains or the words 'In God We Trust' on American coins or religious inscriptions on the official buildings in the nation's capital. Clearly, the modern understanding of the First Amendment would never have given them birth. Yet the religious nature of the nation's enemy, the moral crises of America's soldiers,

and the spiritual passions of the new generation at war may make them more essential to America's military efforts today than ever before. The inconsistencies do not stop there. They wear a uniform but cannot carry a weapon. They receive a check from the state to do the work of the church in a society deathly afraid of the mixture of church and state. They can preach God's will for the individual soul but may not preach God's will for the war. They are ordained by a single religious denomination to preach its truth but as chaplains must tend every possible religious persuasion. [As a result,] the religious nature of their calling often works against them.³

In the midst of the paradoxical world of the military chaplaincy, there are solid legal foundations that make it a valid ministry. The primary legal basis for the existence of the military chaplaincy is that the chaplain's primary purpose is to provide for the First Amendment right to the "free exercise" of religion for all service members, not just those who are of the same faith tradition as the chaplain. As a result, chaplains provide the opportunity to practice, or not practice, religion as an individual choice and style.⁴

It is within this unique context that men and women consider the call to serve their God and Country as chaplains in the Armed Forces of the United States. As I reflect on my last sixteen years of service in the chaplaincy, I clearly see the fingerprints of God throughout this exciting ministry journey. Today, God continues to clarify my own call to serve by allowing me to explore the call to the military chaplaincy among seminary students who aspire to serve as chaplains in the U.S. Armed Forces.

Chaplain Recruiting as an Act of Ministry

In addition to serving as a chaplain for an Air National Guard unit, I enjoy traveling to several colleges and seminaries each year to meet students who have an interest in becoming military chaplains. I also attend various conferences to meet civilian clergy who want to learn more about how they can serve part-time as an Air National Guard chaplain without leaving their full-time civilian ministry vocation.

As a military chaplain recruiter, I have had to develop skills in helping people discern God's call to the military chaplaincy. One of my main functions is to serve as a mentor or coach to those who are trying to discern the call of God in their lives. By offering an open mind and a listening ear, I can provide a dimension of pastoral care in the form of advice and counsel. While mentoring does not generate a call to ministry as a military chaplain, it can certainly be a tool to help shape it. In fact, research shows that seminary students who received mentoring were better prepared to discern their call to vocational ministry. As a result, professors, pastors, and close friends of seminarians can have a tremendous influence in helping define and refine a person's call to ministry.[5]

Additionally, as a chaplain recruiter, I have discovered several key beliefs that help me function in this role. First, I believe God is the one who calls gifted people into the military chaplaincy. According to Chaplains Naomi Paget and Janet McCormack, "The work of the chaplain *begins* with God's call to ministry. Every person experiences God's call in one way or another. It may be the call to saving faith or the call to faithful discipleship. A call to chaplain ministry, however, is a *unique* call, which is *preceded* by a clear call to vocational service in spiritual care."[6]

Recruiting military chaplains is unique in that applicants already sense that God has not only called them to the ministry in general but to the military chaplaincy in particular. Therefore, chaplain recruiting is radically different from other forms of recruiting efforts directed at prospective Soldiers, Sailors, Airmen, Marines, and Coast Guardsmen. However, several challenges remain to recruiting military chaplains.

Regarding the difficulties in military chaplain recruiting, Commander Gary Carr, Navy Recruiting Chaplain program manager, said the following:

> The [Navy] Chaplain Corps is the most difficult program to recruit into. We work within an entirely different demographic. The average age of a pastor today is 44, so America's clergy is getting older. The Navy's upper age limit for clergy is 40, and that makes recruiting very challenging, since we do not begin to see clergy until they are at least 30. The motivating influence for the [Navy] Chaplain Corps recruiters is a desire to find the finest clergy in America who have a sincere call to minister to young people and a commitment of service to country. We are working hard at getting the right material to the right people. We must remain consistent about getting our message out to every possible seminary student in America. In the Navy Chaplain Corps, we provide for those of our own faith group, we facilitate ministry for those of other faith groups, and we care for all.[7]

As a chaplain recruiter, I do not feel the need to persuade seminarians or civilian clergy into becoming military chaplains. Since 1973, when the U.S. ended the military draft, people now choose whether or not they want to enter the U.S. Armed Forces. As a result, the ranks include men and women who want to serve as chaplains because God has called them into this unique vocation. From a theological perspective, God is sovereign over any military chaplain recruiting effort, and in my own experience, aspiring military chaplains often track me down before I find them.

Furthermore, military chaplaincy is radically different from being a pastor of a church. As a result, many gifted seminarians and civilian pastors may not function well within the military setting if God has not called them to this venue. Therefore, my role is that of a sower who scatters the seed about ministry opportunities that exist within the context of the U.S. military. While I may plant the seed, and others come alongside to water it, God is the One ultimately who refines the call as He alone prepares people for this unique mission field (1 Corinthians 3:6-7).

For example, during an interview with the *American Legion* magazine, Army Chaplain John Kenny described how he first sensed a call to military ministry as follows:

> After serving in a church for several years, I felt called to continue to minister but in a different way. In light of 9/11 and the war in Iraq, the idea of being a chaplain seemed like a perfect way for me to continue to serve both my Lord and our nation. My decision to join the Army was cemented on a trip to Washington, D.C. Walking among the memorials, the Capitol and the White House, I was overwhelmed with pride for my country. I believed at that moment God was leading me to serve in the Army chaplaincy.[8]

In the above example, God worked in the midst of the tragedy of 9/11/01 to call a young man into military chaplaincy. This is just one example of how God works throughout history and calls people to serve Him as they also serve their country in the military.

Approaching Chaplain Recruiting as a Participant with God

In reflecting on an article written by Merwyn Johnson,[9] I approach ministry as a chaplain recruiter who is a *participant* in a person's call to ministry. This role is similar to that of a coach or mentor. God alone calls each one, but He invites me to *participate* in helping people discern their call to the military chaplaincy. Unlike other types of military recruiters who often feel pressured to fill a number of slots every month, in the military chaplaincy, there is an understanding and appreciation of the *divine* call to ministry.

Herein lies the distinctly theological activity of the call to military chaplaincy. God has always had a plan for His Kingdom and the Great Commission includes members of the U.S. military. Therefore, the military chaplain is an ordained minister who is called by God to pastor a specific group of people who serve in the U.S. Armed Forces. As a result, military chaplains from the Christian tradition sense a burden to answer the call to chaplaincy in *obedience* to the Great Commission of Jesus Christ to "go and make disciples of all nations" (Matthew 28:19-20).

In many ways, the military chaplain functions as a missionary sent by his or her congregation or faith group to be a witness to the ends of the earth (Acts 1:8). For some, it is a full-time commitment on active duty; for others, it is a part-time commitment in the National Guard or Reserves. In my own situation, I first enlisted in the Air Force as a Chaplain Assistant on active duty, then received a commission as a Chaplain Candidate in the Air Force Reserve, and later became a chaplain in the Air National Guard.

In her extensive research among students, Alice Cullinan surveyed 365 participants about whether they would consider their call to be (1) one that was a gradual, growing conviction that the Lord was leading in that direction, or (2) a specific call at a time and place they could recall. According to this study, 66% said that their calls were gradual, while only 33% said their calls were sudden or occurred at a time they could pinpoint.[10] In my own experience, it was through a unique series of events that God called me into the military chaplaincy over a period of ten years.

When civilian clergy transition from the traditional church pastorate or other ministry to serve as a military chaplain, it is unfortunate that some believe that they have "left the ministry" altogether! Yet, chaplains are ministers of the gospel who wear the uniform of their country, having answered a specialized call of God to provide a shepherd's care to service members. Frequently, though not always, a chaplain's call is influenced by previous military experience, quite often in the enlisted ranks. Therefore, firsthand experience with the intense pressures and urgent needs experienced by service members leads to a keen awareness of what motivated, gifted chaplains can do to help.[11]

Officers Christian Fellowship (OCF) is a Christian organization whose purpose is to glorify God by uniting Christian military officers for Biblical fellowship and outreach, while equipping and encouraging them to minister effectively in the military society. OCF recently interviewed several military chaplains for what advice they would give to someone who was considering becoming a military chaplain

Those who desire to become military chaplains can glean from the following insights into the nature of vocational military ministry:

> There are great opportunities, but the chaplaincy can be one of the *loneliest* positions in a unit. These are *demanding* times of ministry—facing life and death *daily*. God is faithful to supply all of our needs (Phil. 4:19). We are *not called* to a task *without the resources* to accomplish it.

For God and Country: Considering the Call to Military Chaplaincy

It is a *great and noble calling*, and people who have had *prior military service* tend to do best because they can understand and relate to the culture and environment. To be successful, you must be *athletically oriented* and able to keep up with young service members on runs and marches. Get as much *supervised ministry experience* with civilians as possible before becoming a chaplain; performing funerals, counseling, hospital visitation, and preaching. There are *seminary scholarships* of thousands of dollars being offered when you become a "chaplain candidate" during seminary.
Confirm your calling to ministry *in the local church*. Become active in volunteer Christ-centered and Bible-centered ministry. You may think you are called, but the internal call is *only half* of the equation. Is it *confirmed* by God's people as they observe your life within the body of Christ? Read and study the Bible.
Explore and *ask* questions. Be honest about the *probability* of combat deployment. There is a measure of "social work" that will require agile leadership from chaplains to address the human needs of warriors and families—that may not always land them in chapel.[12]

The above advice is priceless to any prospective military chaplain in the process of discerning his or her call to the chaplaincy. It also explains how the call to military chaplaincy involves a definitive interplay among God, the minister, and the church. God is actively at work in the world today and still calls men and women into the adventure of military chaplaincy.

First, God initiates the call to the military chaplaincy. Next, the person is responsible to respond in obedience to His call on his or her life. Then, depending on the personal circumstances at the time of God's call to the military chaplaincy, it may take someone several years to meet the educational, ecclesiastical, and military requirements to become a chaplain. During this process, the endorser of the person's denomination or faith group will help determine if the applicant is fit for service in the military. In this way, the denominational endorsing agency helps confirm or affirm God's call to serve in the military chaplaincy. This process further demonstrates chaplain recruiting as an act of ministry that involves God, the Church, and prospective chaplains.

The traditional approach to full-time ministry, whether in the church or the chaplaincy, is normally to complete graduate theological education, prepare for ordination through an internship or similar program, and obtain ministry/pastoral experience that leads to an endorsement as a military chaplain. Throughout the process of preparing for ministry, God is at work in and through these traditions to help refine the call to the military chaplaincy.

In my own experience, the U.S. military has acknowledged God's call on my life to function as a chaplain within the Armed Forces. In the military setting, the chaplain is called to be a "visible reminder of the Holy." Consequently, the military chaplain often finds him or herself confronted by a set of worldly values that stand in opposition to the Kingdom values of God. Herein lies one of the greatest mission fields in the world due to the ministry setting to which the chaplain is called. The U.S. military certainly comprises one of the largest—but often overlooked—mission fields in the world. One chaplain summed it up by saying, "If ministers of the gospel are called to be Jesus' hands and feet, his voice and arms, and if they carry his strengthening word and healing into all the world—even into such dreadful contexts as armed conflict and war—then, from the Christian perspective, this taking of Jesus into the hell of combat and into the face of death is the most fundamental reason for the military chaplaincy."[13]

I could not agree more with this statement. As a result, this project provided me with the opportunity to reflect on my work as a military chaplain recruiter and further examine the call to the military chaplaincy among a group of seminary students.

The Project Location, Setting, and Situation

The majority of workshop participants involved in this project were seminary students or alumni of Columbia International University (CIU). This institution was birthed by the prayers of Miss Emily Dick, a young woman who taught a Sunday school class in one of the mill villages in Columbia, South Carolina. In 1913, she became concerned for the spiritual and material needs of the workers and their families, so she attended Moody Bible Institute for more training in the Bible. After her return, she realized that a Bible institute in Columbia was needed in order to train those who wanted more Bible education.

In the fall of 1923, Columbia Bible School officially began classes in the Colonia Hotel in downtown Columbia under the teaching of Dr. Robert C. McQuilkin. In 1929, the school began offering four-year bachelor's degrees, and changed its name to Columbia Bible College. The institution began offering graduate degrees in 1936 and became officially recognized as a university in 1994. Today, CIU is comprised of an undergraduate Bible College, Seminary and School of Ministry, and Graduate School.

The campus of CIU is located on 400 scenic acres next to the Broad River, just minutes from the hub of South Carolina's capital city, Columbia. CIU students represent many denominations, ethnic and cultural backgrounds, and reflect the socio-economic diversity of the world—united by their desire to know Christ and to make Him known.

The five core values of CIU are as follows: Authority of Scripture, Victorious Christian Living, World Evangelization, Prayer and Faith, and Evangelical Unity.[14] As an alumnus of CIU (M.Div., 2000) and former board member of the Alumni Association Leadership Council, I desire to help CIU seminary students discern their call to ministry so that they will be better prepared for launching into ministry after graduation.

As a chaplain recruiter, I frequently visit CIU to setup a chaplain recruiting table and speak with students that sense God calling them to the military chaplaincy. Conducting a research project with these students gave them an opportunity to reflect on the military chaplaincy as a vocation. This project also provided students with a means to demonstrate their call to the military chaplaincy. The academic setting of a seminary campus was conducive for engaging students in the process of discerning their call to the ministry in general and the military chaplaincy in particular.

CIU is recognized around the world as a premier institution for preparing foreign missionaries for service. According to Dr. George Murray, Chancellor of the University, CIU produces more missionaries than the combined number of institutions within the Association of Theological Schools. Since the year 2000, graduates from the Bible College, Graduate School, and Seminary go on to serve in the follow categories:

Table 1. Service Location of CIU Alumni, 2000-2008

Percentage	Category
25%	Alumni Serving in a Local Church/Parachurch Ministry
25%	Alumni Serving in Missionary Service
50%	Alumni Serving in the Marketplace

Today, more than 16,000 alumni of CIU serve in Christian ministry in more than 130 countries, and CIU is one of the world's leading missionary and ministry training centers. The seminary and graduate student body at CIU offered a diverse setting to conduct this project. The following table depicts statistics for the spring 2008 semester:

Table 2. CIU Seminary and Graduate School Alumni and Students, May 2008

Number	Category
6337	Graduate School/Seminary Alumni
447	Current Graduate/Seminary Students
252	Current Male Graduate/Seminary Students
195	Current Female Graduate/Seminary Students
32	Average Age of Master's Level Students
49	Average Age of Doctoral Level Students
20	Countries Represented in Graduate/Seminary Students
40	Denominations Represented among Graduate/Seminary Students
16	Graduate/Seminary Degree Programs Offered
34	Graduate/Seminary Faculty Members
132	Current M.Div. Students Enrolled
238	Current M.A. Programs Students Enrolled
16	Current D.Min. Students Enrolled
61	Other Non-Degree Seeking Students Enrolled

When I was a student at CIU, I knew of only two other students who were preparing to enter the military chaplaincy. Among this small group of prospective military chaplains, one of our concerns was that no courses were offered in military chaplaincy or institutional ministry. In 2008, CIU had twelve seminary students who were preparing to serve as military chaplains after graduation.

However, no chaplaincy courses existed for these seminary students to take as electives. As a result, this project met an immediate need for those seminary students who were considering the call to the military chaplaincy.

In the year 2010, the Army, Navy, and Air Force chaplain schools will be co-located at Fort Jackson in Columbia, South Carolina. As a result, CIU projects that it may attract more students interested in their degree programs who desire to become military chaplains. CIU is considering the option to offer some new elective courses to help M.Div. students prepare for ministry in the military chaplaincy. Accordingly, I would like to serve CIU in the future as an adjunct faculty member for developing and teaching courses that would help prepare students for ministry as military chaplains.

Revised edition note: It is important to note that CIU Seminary and School of Ministry did establish a thriving ATS accredited Chaplaincy degree program in July 2011 which was pioneered by Dr. Michael Langston, CAPT, CHC, USN, (Ret.). More information about this program is contained in Appendix I.

According to several professors, there are more students enrolled in the 2007-2008 school year who are interested in the military chaplaincy than ever before. Therefore, this situation presented me with an opportunity to conduct a D.Min. research project in this particular academic setting that would assist prospective military chaplains discern their call to ministry.

According to the 2007-2008 Annual Report, CIU has over 16,000 total alumni (includes undergraduate students) serving in the world as professional Christians in the ministry as well as Christian professionals in the marketplace. This report provided a breakdown of the *location* of ministry and type of *organization* that students desire to serve. The following tables depict the vocational goals of 230 recent graduates.

Table 3. Graduating Student's Vocational Goals by Location of Service, May 2008

Percent	Location of Service
23%	Vocational Christian Service *outside* the USA/Canada
18%	Vocational Christian Service *inside* the USA/Canada
13%	Vocational Christian Service location undecided
14%	Undecided
11%	Marketplace
8%	Tentmaker location undecided
7%	Tentmaker outside the USA/Canada
3%	Tentmaker inside the USA/Canada

Table 4. Graduating Student's Vocational Goals by Organization, May 2008

Percent	Type of Organization
28%	Mission Agency/Overseas
20%	Church inside the USA/Canada
15%	Marketplace Organization
11%	Other Christian Organization
9%	Other
7%	Educational Organization
4%	Evangelistic/Discipleship
4%	No Organization
2%	Home Mission inside the USA/Canada

The Project's Purpose

The purpose of this project was to examine the call to military chaplaincy among current seminary students and recent graduates of CIU.

The Project's Goals

The two goals of this project are directly related to its ultimate purpose. The goals chosen helped students discern and demonstrate their call to serve as military chaplains. In addition, as a chaplain recruiter, these goals helped me understand the reasons why students wanted to become military chaplains. Both goals were measured and evaluated at the conclusion of the project and were reported in a separate chapter. The goals I set out to accomplish in this project were as follows:

<u>Goal for Seminary Students</u> (As Workshop Participants)
1. To be able to discern and demonstrate a clear call to the military chaplaincy.

<u>Goal for the Minister</u> (As a Military Chaplain Recruiter)
1. To list and interpret the common demographic factors and vocational motivations of a group of seminary students called to serve as military chaplains.

The Details of the Project

In order to achieve the stated purpose and goals of this project, I engaged a group of fifteen students in a workshop about the call to military chaplaincy. Of these fifteen individuals, eight were current students at CIU, three were alumni of CIU, two were prospective students at CIU, and one was enrolled at another seminary. Several CIU faculty members helped me identify students who had an interest in becoming military chaplains. After making initial contact with these students and alumni, they agreed to participate in the project in order to better understand their own call to the military chaplaincy.

This project took place off campus from the end of March to the middle of April 2008. Participants initially completed a "Prospective Military Chaplain Survey" that was designed to be taken online at the Question Pro website.[15] Following this survey, most students participated in a three-session small group workshop that was developed and called "Consider the Call: Prospective Military Chaplain Workshop."[16]

Participants received the questionnaires to answer for each session and background readings as email attachments two weeks prior to each small group discussion. They typed their responses in the Microsoft Word document that was emailed to them and brought a copy of their responses to each small group discussion session. The participants were encouraged to keep all of their workshop materials in a notebook for further study and reflection.

The group met for one hour on Wednesday afternoons at a conference room off campus. I served as the workshop facilitator for each discussion and encouraged participants to interact with each other about their call to ministry as a military chaplain. I obtained their permission to audio record each discussion which helped me later capture important insights to include in this project/dissertation. I also copied their written responses to a spreadsheet to look for common themes, issues, and concerns that helped me further analyze and interpret the data.

Conclusion

Considering the call to ministry can be a difficult process for any seminary student. When someone senses a call to ministry outside the traditional church setting, such as the military chaplaincy, there can be a greater deal of difficulty in discerning the call. As a result, the author designed a vocational workshop to help a group of seminary students discern a call to the military chaplaincy. In the remaining chapters of this project dissertation, the author explores the call to military chaplaincy as an act of ministry that involves an initial call from God, the confirmation of the Church, and the obedience of the person who says, "Here am I, send me" (Isaiah 6:8b).

Chapter two overviews relevant literature that informed the project regarding the norms of the call to ministry, the functions of conducting the project in a small group format, and the current context of the military chaplaincy. Chapter three discusses the Biblical and theological insights into the call to military chaplaincy as a vocation by examining several Biblical texts that relate to the various aspects of the military chaplaincy and provide a Biblical basis for ministry.

Chapter four explores the call to military chaplaincy from the research data gleaned from a group of seminary students who demonstrated a clear call to the chaplaincy by participating in the "Consider the Call Prospective Military Chaplain Workshop." In addition, the author, who also helps recruit military chaplains, lists and interprets common factors and vocational motivations of students called to serve as military chaplains.

In conclusion, chapter five examines the outcomes of the project and how it can benefit military chaplain recruiters, vocational counselors, denominational endorsers of military chaplains, and any person who is exploring or considering the military chaplaincy as a future vocation.

CHAPTER 2

CHAPLAIN LITERATURE REVIEW

Introduction

This project focused on helping seminary students at CIU discern and demonstrate their call to serve as military chaplains after graduation. The Biblical aspects of this project focused on specific scriptures that provided themes and insights into the call to ministry of military chaplains that serve outside the context of the local church. The theological aspects of this project dealt with the matter of "calling" or "vocation." In researching available literature, one will find several excellent resources that deal with the norms of this project by addressing the Biblical, theological, and historical aspects of the call to ministry.

Literature on the Norms of the Call to Ministry

In conjunction with the ongoing work of the Programs for the Theological Exploration of Vocation, William Placher provided an excellent book that covers twenty centuries of Christian wisdom on the matter of vocation.[1] In *Callings*, Placher informed the research of this project dissertation by listing the key Biblical texts regarding the call of particular individuals in the Old and New Testaments. Included in this list are Abraham, Moses,

Deborah, Samuel, Isaiah, Jeremiah, and Mary, the mother of Jesus, the disciples of Jesus, Philip, and Saul. In the rest of the book, Placher provided an overview of the "call" and "vocation" during the following four historical periods.

These periods are the Early Church (100-500), the Middle Ages (500-1500), after the Reformation (1500-1800), and in the post-Christian world (1800-present). Placher's book further informed the project by providing direct quotes from fifty influential persons within the Christian tradition which helps readers understand the theology of vocation and its development over the last twenty centuries. This book helped with conducting historical research into the theology of the call to ministry.

In a classic work entitled *The Call to Prophetic Service*,[2] one finds an excellent treatment of the Biblical call of the prophets. In this book, Henry Schaeffer examined the conditions under which each of the prophets were called, the method God used to convey the call, the response to the call, obedience to the call, and the message each prophet was inspired to deliver. This book is more than a discussion of the experience of the call to ministry. It also contained a thorough treatment of the message and mission of the one called and commissioned for a specific task. As a result, this book provided insights into the study of the Biblical characters whom God called to the prophetic ministry. This book also helped inform the Biblical norm of the military chaplain to function in a *prophetic* ministry within the culturally *pluralistic* military environment. Like the prophet Nathan was to King David, there are times when military chaplains will need to speak the truth in love while advising senior civilian and military officials. The prophetic role of chaplains can be minimized or marginalized by the institution they are serving, but chaplains are called by God to stand up to evil and injustice wherever it occurs. As a result, this project discussed the importance of the prophetic call of chaplains in the military environment.

Written with the average American college student in mind, Douglas Schuurman takes an ecumenical and ethical approach to the matter of calling in his book, *Vocation: Discerning our Callings in Life*.[3] This book informed this project by providing a historical look at the call to ministry through the historical lens of the doctrine of vocation. The purpose of Schuurman's book is to develop a contemporary articulation of the classic Protestant doctrine of vocation so that people can understand how God has gifted them for a particular calling in life. Schuurman's work offers insights from the minds of key theologians such as Martin Luther, John Calvin, Karl Barth, and Dietrich Bonhoeffer.

In tracing the historical traditions concerning vocation, the author makes a strong case for the reader to examine the Biblical roots of the doctrine of vocation within the Protestant, Roman Catholic, and Orthodox churches. Thus, readers can glean further insights from this book when researching the Biblical texts and the theological aspects of the call to ministry. This book further informed this project by emphasizing the need to rediscover one's Christian identity in a world that threatens Christian belief and practice by focusing on selfish individualism that glorifies man instead of the selfless service that glories God.

Alice Cullinan, author of *Sorting it Out: Discerning God's Call to Ministry*,[4] helps Christians discern their call to ministry by engaging them in a series of self-evaluation questions that can be used for individual or small group study. Her book primarily addressed students of Christian colleges, Bible schools, and seminaries who are in the process of discerning the specific vocation that God has called them to serve.

This book helped with the development of the Consider the Call workshop questionnaires for prospective military chaplains. The book also informed this project by providing insights into *defining* a call to ministry, *experiencing* a call to ministry, and *discerning* God's call to ministry. Cullinan's book contains important data gathered from her extensive research with 365 participants who desired more clarity in understanding God's call to ministry. This project included insightful quotations from her research that supported the data gathered from participants in the Consider the Call workshop.

In *Hearing God's Call: Ways of Discernment for Clergy and Laity*,[5] Ben Johnson offered experience-based insights into the process of discerning if a call is truly from God or not. Unlike other books written on the call to ministry, Johnson also addressed the role of the laity who do not serve in vocational Christian ministry but volunteer their time, talents, and resources within their church. This book is comprised of many inspiring stories of persons who came to Johnson for help concerning the divine call. As a result, this book informed the overall design of the Consider the Call workshop by allowing time within the small group discussion sessions for students to openly share their stories of *how* God led them to seminary and *why* they were specifically pursuing the military chaplaincy as a vocation. Through sharing their stories, both verbally and in written form, all workshop participants were better able to demonstrate a clear call to the military chaplaincy. This book also provided a thoughtful series of discernment exercises at the end of each chapter and included an appendix that examined the call of prominent Biblical figures.

Literature on the Functions of Conducting the Project

There is a wealth of literature related to the functions of choosing a project topic of interest, conducting the project, employing research methods, and evaluating the project. In selecting a project idea, I found John Creswell's book entitled *Educational Research*[6] to be extremely helpful. Creswell's research guided me in a process of thought that caused me to narrow down my topic into a central purpose statement and goals. In *Research Design*,[7] a companion book by Creswell, I learned about various methods in conducting both qualitative and quantitative research. Both of these books helped me understand the importance of research as part of my project.

In designing tools for conducting qualitative and quantitative research, I found the following two books by Arlene Fink to be of value: *How to Ask Survey Questions*[8] and *How to Conduct Surveys*.[9] Since the purpose of my project was to examine the call to the military chaplaincy among a small group of seminary students, I needed to design an intake survey and list of open-ended questions for the small group workshop sessions. These books provided me with some sample surveys and guidelines for using these tools in an academic setting.

An excellent resource to planning and evaluating projects within religious organizations is entitled *Projects That Matter*.[10] In this book, Cahalan introduced the five basic elements of project design and a six-step process for project implementation and evaluation. I found this book helpful in choosing the overall purpose for my project and goals for the students and myself as a researcher.

Finally, regarding the functions of being a facilitator for a small group workshop, I used the insights gleaned from several books by Neil McBride. In his book, *How to Lead Small Groups,*[11] McBride explained the process of leading a small group, dealing with group dynamics, presentation methods, learning styles, serving as a facilitator, coping with conflict, and evaluating group progress and outcomes. In his companion book, *How to Have Great Small Group Meetings,*[12] McBride covered tips for planning for success, increasing participation, using humor, variety, and spontaneity. Both books were assets to carrying out my project in a small group setting.

Literature on the Context of the Military Chaplaincy

In conducting research on the context of current understanding of "the call" or "vocation," I found a wealth of books on the general "call to ministry" for a pastoral candidate that is preparing ministry in the local church setting. However, there is a lack of other literature regarding the call to a *specialized* ministry setting, such as the military chaplaincy. However, what I did locate was in the form of internet sources, news articles, and several books that I will summarize in the following pages.

It is no secret that there is a massive shortage of military chaplains today and the media has highlighted the growing problem over the last few years. In a recent story reported by *ABC News,* Army chaplains conceded that their job description is not exactly attractive to many people. The pay is not great, the conditions are grueling, and the demands are the kind that leaves a body and soul drained at the end of a day. Yet, they believe many are called to the chaplaincy, and that it is not just a job, but a vocation.

The article informed the research for this project by explaining how some soldiers are sensing a call into the military chaplaincy from the battlefields of war. For Army Reserve Chaplain (CPT) Katie Knapp, it was her own need as a soldier, in a camp just outside of Baghdad, which prompted her to enter seminary and attend the Army chaplain school. She saw the effects of the chaplain shortage that was already a problem when she was in Iraq. "I felt I was very technically proficient in my tasks, but I was spiritually empty. I was allowed one hour a week to go to worship services, and sometimes I had to fight for that hour a week."[13] Knapp now proudly serves as an Army Chaplain.

Another article in *USA Today* documented the shortage of chaplains in the Army Reserve and National Guard. According to Chaplain (LTC) Ran Dolinger, the Army Reserves are short more than 100 chaplains of an authorized 516 and the Army National Guard needs nearly 250 more chaplains to fill its 722 slots. The article informed the research of this project by revealing the growing difficulty in recruiting younger, fully qualified clergy to enter the military chaplaincy.

In fact, to persuade more ministers to enter the military, the Guard started a special recruiting program two years ago. Recruiters look for prospects at church conferences, seminaries and major ministries. The Guard offers new chaplains a $10,000 signing bonus and $20,000 to repay student loans. There is also a $30,000 bonus for chaplains who stay in for a second six-year tour. The article concludes with a quotation from Army National Guard Chaplain David White who said, "We go where we are called to be. If God calls us to go into a war zone, we go because that's where the soldier is."[14]

In a well-documented book, Doris Bergen examines the work of military chaplains and the development of the military chaplaincy from a historical and geographic perspective in *The Sword of the Lord: Military Chaplains for the First to the Twenty-First Century*.[15] This unique book documented the work of the clergy serving within governmental and military settings during the pre-Christian era in the Roman Empire up to the second half of the twentieth century. This is the first book to examine the work of military chaplains in Europe and North America from Christian and Jewish faith traditions. As a result, this book informed this project by providing details into the ministry of Rabbi Max Wall during World War II and Father Joseph O'Donnell during the Vietnam War. These personal stories described their call to ministry and their ministry to service members during wartime.

Reading these inspiring accounts influenced the design of the Consider the Call workshop by encouraging seminary students to participate by sharing their journey to the military chaplaincy. This book is the most comprehensive authority available on the origins and development of military chaplaincy from the first to the twenty-first century.

In his autobiography, *A Table in the Presence*,[16] Navy Chaplain Carey Cash chronicled his journey into the chaplaincy and ministry with the first group of Marines that crossed into Iraq. This book informed this project as an excellent resource to give any person who is sensing an inward or outward call to the military chaplaincy. In Carey's situation, God used his experience at a military college, specific scriptures, and a member of his extended family (who was also a chaplain) to help define his call to the chaplaincy. As I designed my prospective military chaplain survey, I was interested if other chaplains' call to ministry involved some of these factors as well. Hence, I included several questions about the different elements of the call and types of people who may have been influential.

For God and Country: Considering the Call to Military Chaplaincy

In a special guide for churches and chaplains, Donald Hadley and Gerald Richards lay a firm foundation for the military chaplaincy in *Ministry with the Military*.[17] As a resource to this project, the opening chapters of this handbook provided key insights into how the military system operates, attitudes for ministry in a pluralistic setting, the role of chaplains, the legitimacy of the military chaplaincy, and the Biblical foundations for ministry within the U.S. Armed Forces.

Although published over fifteen years ago, the message of this book is relevant to any person who is considering a call to the military chaplaincy or presently serves as a chaplain. The Appendix section provided statistical information on U.S. military personnel that helped determine the demographic data categories that I needed to include in my own research. Overall, this book is an excellent primer for the clergy member who becomes a chaplain without any prior military service.

In a unique book, written after visiting troops serving at home and abroad, historian Stephen Mansfield explored how the War on Terror is affecting the spiritual life and beliefs of our troops. In *The Faith of the American Soldier*,[18] Mansfield examined what goes through the mind of an American warrior spiritually when facing the enemy. This book informed this project by helping me understand the current ministry setting in which military chaplains function. Mansfield sees a new generation of military personnel who are entering the military without any connection to a particular church or denomination. As a result, a new brand of spirituality that is eclectic and relational is permeating throughout the military ranks. Through personal interviews and observations with this young generation of "millennials," Mansfield revealed the new challenges chaplains face as they strive to remain faithful to their calling, ordination vows, and the faith group they represent.

In his compelling autobiography, *Supernatural Events in the Life of an Ordinary Man*,[19] retired Chaplain (COL) Jim Ammerman explained his call to the chaplaincy as a young teenager in 1938 and documented the amazing acts of ministry while serving as an Army Chaplain for 23 years. After he retired, Ammerman founded the Chaplaincy of Full Gospel Churches (CFGC), which is an endorsing agency for military, healthcare, correctional, and corporate chaplains.

This autobiography informed the project by explaining how God calls ordinary men and women to do extraordinary acts of ministry for His glory. Ammerman's call to the military chaplaincy involved several types of "burning bush" experiences with God.

In my prospective chaplain survey, I wanted to know if other chaplains had similar divine encounters with God in their call. As a result, I asked participants to describe how they experienced of the call to ministry.

Chaplains Naomi Paget and Janet McCormack explored the vocation of chaplaincy within healthcare, correctional, workplace, military, first-responder (police, firefighter, emergency medical service), and other settings in *The Work of the Chaplain*.[20] This unique book introduced the concept that the work of Christian chaplains is an extension of Christ's ministry to all people.

Paget and McCormack covered the foundations for chaplaincy by addressing the historical and legal aspects of ministry outside the walls of the church and provided a solid Biblical basis for chaplaincy as a valid vocation. This book challenged me to dig into the Scriptures to discover the Biblical themes and insights that relate to the various roles of military chaplains. The book also informed the project by exploring the various roles of the chaplain by defining specific ministry tasks and competencies for each chaplain to demonstrate.

The appendix provided insights into how prospective chaplains can prepare themselves for this unique ministry by understanding their vocational call, obtaining the necessary theological training, participating in clinical training, working towards ordination, and applying for an endorsement. This superb book provides specific guidance to prospective chaplains.

During my research, I also discovered several dissertations that were related to the call to ministry. These dissertations were authored by those pursuing doctoral degrees in education, ministry, and philosophy. The first dissertation that sparked my interest was *The Relationship Between Mentoring and Seminarians Called Into Full-Time Vocational Ministry*.[21] The purpose of this study was to examine the relationship between mentoring and God's call into vocational ministry by way of analyzing perceptions generated from a mentor survey as well as personality traits derived from a temperament sorter. This study challenged me to question prospective military chaplains about the types of persons who had an influence on them becoming chaplains. I also wanted to know if the prospective chaplains I surveyed had ever been involved in mentoring, guiding, or recruiting someone who became a military chaplain. Accordingly, this dissertation provided insight into the two goals that I chose for my own project.

Another project dissertation I found helpful was titled, *What is the Call to Ministry?*[22] by John Womack, Sr. This project dissertation used a twelve-question interview process to gather insights from a select group of African-American pastors who were leading urban congregations. This study gave me several insights into the types of background questions I needed to include in my military chaplain survey. This well-written dissertation also addressed the Biblical themes on the different types of calls to the ministry, such as the general, internal, and external call. The appendix also described the author's call to ministry, which was a beneficial resource to my study.

Concerning the perceived role of the military chaplain, I found an informative dissertation written by Army Chaplain Will Ghere about the perceived role of the military chaplain.[23] His project contained several evaluations that helped me prepare the background demographic data that I needed to ask in my military chaplain survey. Ghere's study also provided insight into how a chaplain would determine job satisfaction as related to his or her call to ministry. As a result, my chaplain survey included a question that related to this particular issue. Consequently, Chaplain Ghere's research data provided guidance into the design of my prospective military chaplain survey.

Finally, an excellent resource I found was a set of position papers published by the Division of Chaplains of the United Methodist Church in 1979.[24] This study was in response to a petition to the General Conference of the United Methodist Church.

The petition requested that the Conference take immediate steps to disengage the church from the military chaplaincy system and replace it with a civilian chaplaincy, whereby ministers would be appointed to serve military personnel without themselves becoming members of the military establishment. The petition also sought the cooperation of other denominations and even threatened to withdraw all United Methodist chaplains from the military.

In response to this petition, a church leader wrote an excellent treatise on the call to service as a military chaplain. This paper noted that the Great Commission to "go into all the world" included all military personnel and concluded by stating that if United Methodist chaplains were withdrawn from the military altogether, then other Protestant chaplains would be responsible for the pastoral care of United Methodists in the military. As a result, this paper informed the design of the prospective military chaplain survey by including questions regarding the importance of providing spiritual care to members of their own denomination as well as those from other Christian traditions and faith groups.

Conclusion

In the past, there has been a shortage of literature written about the call to ministry of military chaplains. However, as colleges and seminaries begin to offer courses on military chaplaincy, scholarly books are being published for academic use. These pieces of literature often discuss the circumstances surrounding the initial call to serve God and Country in the military chaplaincy.

Furthermore, as military personnel[25] and chaplains[26] return from deployments in the warzones of Afghanistan and Iraq, some are taking time to reflect and write about their service and ministry overseas. There are also several books written in the last decade by retired chaplains who took time to reflect on the various roles of military chaplains. One such book is *The Chaplain: Fighting the Bullets*,[27] by Charles Grooms, a retired chaplain of the South Carolina State Guard.

A final excellent resource to any aspiring military chaplain is *Voices of Chaplaincy*,[28] edited by retired Navy Rear Admiral, Chaplain David White, former Executive Director of the Military Chaplains Association of the United States of America. This book is a compilation of wisdom and guidance from former military Chiefs of Chaplains and senior chaplains who provide valuable insights to those preparing themselves for service in the unique calling of military chaplaincy. This book informed this research project by examining the many different roles of the military chaplain such as, pastor, preacher, priest, staff officer, caregiver, and ethical leader. In the next chapter, I will discuss some of these roles and provide a Biblical basis for the military chaplaincy as a vocation..

CHAPTER 3

BIBLICAL INSIGHTS INTO THE CALL TO MILITARY CHAPLAINCY

Introduction

It is a sad commentary against humanity that only about 268 years of over 3,350 years of recorded history have been free of war. The existence of war is a complex moral problem that must be confronted by churches and society alike. As revealed in James 4:1-2, the source of war is *sin*: "Where do wars and fights come *from among you*? Do they not come *from your desires* for pleasure that war *in your members*? *You lust* and do not have. *You murder* and *covet* and cannot obtain. *You fight* and *war* ..."(NKJV, emphasis mine).

While all of creation yearns for a world free from war, Jesus promised that war would be an earthly reality until His return. "But when you hear of wars and rumors of wars, do not be troubled; for such things *must happen*, but the end is not yet. For nation *will rise* against nation, and kingdom against kingdom. And there *will be* earthquakes in various places, and there *will be* famines and troubles. These are the beginnings of sorrows" (Mark 13:7-8, NKJV, emphasis mine).

The reality is that war exists and is here to stay as history has well documented throughout the centuries. As philosophers, theologians, and politicians have discovered over time, there are *no* easy answers to war.

However, the focus of this chapter is *not* to survey the various positions on "just war theory" or "conscientious objections" to military service. Rather the author will draw out several passages that provide Biblical insights into the call to military chaplaincy. The author writes from a Christian perspective and holds the premise that the vocation of military chaplaincy is a high and honorable calling from God to provide pastoral care to U.S. service members who have the constitutional right to the free exercise of religion. As a result, the author views Christian chaplains who serve in the military as an extension of Christ's ministry to all people. The following Biblical texts relate to the various aspects of the call to military chaplaincy and provide a Biblical basis for ministry.

A Call to Lifestyle Evangelism
(Matthew 5:13-16)

God leads many Christians to join the military—not just as chaplains—but in other occupations in order to live their lives in such as way that they serve as a witness to the good news of Jesus Christ. Scripture provides insights into the concept of lifestyle evangelism. According to the Gospel of Matthew, when Jesus saw the crowds, he went up on a mountainside and sat down. When his disciples came to him, he began to teach them by saying:

> You are the salt of the earth. But if the salt loses its saltiness, how can it be made salty again? It is no longer good for anything, except to be thrown out and trampled by men. You are the light of the world. A city on a hill cannot be hidden.
> Neither do people light a lamp and put it under a bowl. Instead they put it on its stand, and it gives light to

everyone in the house. In the same way, let your light shine before men, that they may see your good deeds and praise your Father in heaven. (Matthew 5:13-16, NIV)

The military environment provides Christians with countless opportunities to be "salt" and "light" to people who have never heard the gospel or may have never previously attended church. As someone once said, your life may be the only 'Bible' that someone will ever read. In commenting on the principle of lifestyle evangelism in this passage, Joseph Aldrich says, "I think it is fair to say that the majority of Christians have lost their ability to relate significantly to non-Christians. By no stretch of the imagination can the Christian community be called the 'salt of the earth.'

For salt to be effective, it must get *out* of its container and *into* the world of hurting, dying, suffering, sinning people." He goes on to say, "Christians are to *be* the good news before they *share* the good news. The words of the gospel are to be incarnated before they are verbalized."[1] The insights of Aldrich parallel the words of Saint Francis of Assisi when he said, "Preach the gospel always, and if necessary use words." Overall, the military offers a fitting environment where a Christian chaplain can practice lifestyle evangelism.

A Call to Missionary Service
(Matthew 28:19-20; Acts 1:8)

The U.S. military comprises one of the largest—but often overlooked—mission fields in the world. In many ways, military people serve in a culture that is foreign to civilians as Rick Bereit explains in a guidebook for Christians serving in the military.

The military has its own rules, values, and language. It demands more order, structure, and conformity than civilian life. The military, unlike other jobs, is not something you show up to periodically. You don't work *for* the military; you're *in it!* It is a way of life that envelopes you. It makes demands on your abilities, time, and, unlike most professions, your life! When you join the military, you swear to surrender your life, if necessary, in defense of your country. Life-and-death responsibilities accompany the privilege of serving in the military, making it a profession like no other.[2]

It is within this unique context of military life that civilians consider joining the U.S. Armed Forces as a Soldier, Sailor, Airman, Marine, or Coast Guardsman. For example, the following story depicts the inspiring journey of a young man called to military service—not as a chaplain—but as a Marine who happened to be a Christian:

> On a charcoal-black April night, with his future weighing heavily on him, Rano Mariotti sought solitude at the historic battlefield of Gettysburg—the same place in Pennsylvania where thousands of brave soldiers gave their lives 144 years ago. He could almost hear their voices and the thunder of cannons as he stood on the open field, not far from Little Round Top. Though the place was eerie at night, Rano hoped the hallowed spot would help him make a big decision. He was on a retreat with Military Ministry [of Campus Crusade for Christ], and they had been studying the battle of Gettysburg. Rano admired the valor of the more than 7,000 soldiers who gave their lives over a three-day period. 'All men want to be courageous,' he says. 'It's what every man hopes he would be.' While Rano sat at the memorial spot, the place spoke to his heart. His future started to become clear. He decided to go for it—to become a Marine. Believing it was God's plan for him but

not knowing exactly how God would use him, he knew that he could no longer fight this desire.[3]

In the same way, seminary students and civilian clergy have considered the call to the military chaplaincy as a unique vocation. In many respects, the call to military chaplaincy is a call to missionary service. Bereit provides the following missional insights for Christians considering serving in the military as chaplains:

> God has called men and women in every walk of life to live obedient lives among our peers. When we do this, we reflect the life of Jesus, a shining light in a dark world. Jesus said, 'Go and make disciples of all nations' (Matthew 28:19). His command requires going into every nation, but it also implies reaching into every walk of life. That includes the military.[4]

Furthermore, Christians serving in the military can fulfill the mandate of Jesus stated in Acts 1:8 as they receive power to be His witnesses wherever they are sent to serve.

While a seminary student at CIU, I enjoyed discussing my call to ministry with a fellow seminarian who had previously served as a foreign missionary but now desired to serve as a military chaplain. He graduated a few years before I did and joined the Army prior to the September 11, 2001 terrorist attacks. He recently took the time to reflect on his call to the military chaplaincy as he shared his personal journey in the CIU Alumni magazine. The following quotations provide key insights into the relationship between missionary service and military service:

Biblical Insights into the Call to Military Chaplaincy

During an intense season of prayer and fasting *while serving as a missionary* in Albania, I received God's call to the chaplaincy. Although I had prior military service, this call came as a complete shock as I had never considered that the chaplaincy might be a legitimate fulfillment of a boyhood calling to serve Christ *as a cross-cultural missionary*. In fact, previously, I had never felt more out of place than during my period of active service with the U.S. Army. For that reason, I initially dismissed the call altogether, and then when the call began to crystallize, made the decision to apply for the Air Force chaplaincy which I felt was culturally a better fit for me in terms of disposition and gifting. However, hours before submitting my Air Force application, I heard God's voice challenging me, "David, do you think your lifelong preparation has been to prepare you to enjoy an easy life? Get back in the Army." I knew from that moment on, that God was calling me to the *challenges* of Army culture and ministry. I mention the circumstances of my original calling as a chaplain because *that call has made all the ensuing challenges so much easier to handle.* [As a result] I have spent three of the last five years entirely separated from my wife, and my four young children. Over the past five years I have grown to be a huge advocate of chaplain ministry in the Army. At U.S. government expense, the Army asks me to serve its soldiers by providing spiritual direction, life coaching, and moral and ethical guidance. I have unrestricted access to some of our society's most broken members, as well as its future leaders. I am an insider in this ministry. Sharing the daily drudgery, danger, and joy, I live among the lost and the faithful *with a matchless opportunity* to speak into their lives and love them in Christ's name. Additionally, the high profile that the war has received has been a catalyst for the vast numbers of Christians to take an invaluable prayer interest in the ministry. I imagine that only eternity will reveal the movements and grace that this prayer [has produced].[5]

Accordingly, the military chaplaincy relates to missionary service because ministry is conducted within a diversity of cultures that need to be crossed in order be effective.

A Call to be a Friend of Sinners (Matthew 11:19) and Minister to the Needy (Matthew 25:31-46)

Throughout the Gospels, we learn how Jesus went out of His way to cultivate relationships with the outcasts of society such as tax collectors, drunkards, prostitutes, and lepers. Because Jesus shared meals and socialized with such outcasts, religious leaders labeled him as a 'friend of sinners' (Matthew 11:19). The military chaplaincy offers ministry to people who may never again darken the doors of a church because they once had a unpleasant experience with a minister or someone within the church.

Brennan Manning once said that, "The single greatest cause for atheism in the world today are Christians who acknowledge Jesus with their lips and then walk out the door and deny Him by their lifestyle. That is what an unbelieving world simply finds unbelievable."[6] However, people who have witnessed religious hypocrisy in society still have a need for a friend to care for their soul. Consequently, the military chaplain can become such a friend to lost souls by bringing God *to* people where they are at, whether it is in a hospital, a foxhole, on a flight line, or at Fort Leavenworth military prison.

In Matthew 25:31-46, Jesus states that ministry provided to the "least of these" includes those who are hungry, thirsty, strangers, unclothed, sick, and imprisoned. As a result, when clergy leave their comfort zones within the church building and provide ministry to people often located *outside* of the church context, such ministry is performed as if one is serving Jesus Himself. The importance of being a "friend to sinners" and providing ministry to "the least of these" is the Biblical example for taking ministry to where people "are" instead of waiting for them to come inside the church for help.

Commenting on the Matthew 25 passage, Chaplains Naomi Paget and Janet McCormack explain how the text speaks to the chaplain of "the innate worth of *all* persons, not just those who agree with their religion, share their culture, or look like them. Because we are all 'created in the image of God' (Genesis 1:27), we are all entitled to, and worthy of, compassionate ministry and respect. No one is outside of the love or concern of God (John 3:16). Chaplains follow God's example by loving and caring for each person."[7]

A Call to a Ministry of Presence
(Luke 24:13-35)

The cornerstone of the military chaplaincy is the ministry of *presence*. Military chaplains often provide ministry by walking around, visiting military personnel in their workplace. In my own experience as a military chaplain, a primary function during my National Guard training weekend is to build strong relationships with the members of my unit so that I can serve them in their time of need. While spending time with airmen on the flight line, in maintenance back shops, and in administrative offices I get to know them personally, as well as learn of their struggles.

One of the differences of providing ministry outside the context of the four walls of the institutional church is the opportunity to build strong bonds with the troops over time. Commenting on this unique aspect of the chaplaincy, an Army chaplain said, "Because [active duty] chaplains are ministering to the same people seven days a week, spiritual bonds grow more quickly. In a regular [civilian] congregation, one might see parishioners once or twice a week. But during [military] deployments, there are often dozens of services for different denominations during the weekends, as well as Bible studies and counseling services weekly."[8]

As military chaplains build friendships with troops in their unit, they become better prepared to serve them in time of need. The Gospel of Luke records the ministry of presence that Jesus provided when He spent hours walking *with* two men on the road to Emmaus (Luke 24). In the same way, military chaplains are called to be with and walk alongside those dealing with pain, suffering, and grief as they provide a ministry of presence in the U.S. Armed Forces.

Luke 24:15 records how "Jesus himself came up and walked along with them." Likewise, military chaplains are called to walk *with and alongside* troops on the journey of life. Luke 24:17 states that Jesus asked them, "What are you discussing together as you walk along?" Again, military chaplains can take the time to ask the right questions and then *just listen* to military personnel share from their pain. According to federal law and military regulations, the military chaplain is the *only* person granted absolute confidentiality in matters discussed with military members.

The phrase "tell it to the chaplain" is a popular way to explain the provision for military members to talk openly about a personal problem without it getting out to the chain of command. The ministry of presence in just listening to others, is of vital importance to the emotional health and mental stability of military personnel in times of peace and war.

Finally, in Luke 24:27 it is recorded that, "Beginning with Moses and all the Prophets, He [Jesus] explained to them the Scriptures." In the same way, military chaplains have an opportunity to open up God's Word as a source of strength and comfort to warriors. As a result, the example of Jesus in Luke 24 provides a model for military chaplains as they offer a ministry of presence among military personnel. In his personal memoir on serving as a Catholic Chaplain during the Vietnam War, Father Joseph O'Donnell made the following reflections:

> Being a chaplain in the military is not all about war, blood, and guts. Much of the chaplain's work is the same as that of any parish priest. Not every minister, priest, or rabbi is suited to be in institutional ministry, especially in ministry where there can be Violence. If I were choosing chaplains, I would look for three qualities. The first is that he or she should have the ability *to listen*, to listen not only to words, but to, and with, both heart and soul. The ability to listen includes the willingness to *accept people* where they are in their own understanding of life and faith, *not* where the chaplain would like them to be. The second requirement is that the chaplain be *credible*. I have to *live* what I *believe*. I have to be a person of faith, and hope, and love—yes, love—in the midst of war. Credibility is *not a given* in the military, as it may be in civilian churches or denominational institutions. One earns his or her place by *being there*, by listening, by keeping secrets, by speaking when it is time to speak, and not speaking when it is not. The third requirement is that a chaplain understands the nature of *confidentiality*, or Rule of Privilege, as it is called in the *Manual for Courts Martial*, the operative, judicial portion of the Uniform Code of Military Justice. As a chaplain, I have to know *when* to keep my mouth shut.[9]

O'Donnell's insights into the requirements of prospective chaplains closely parallel the ministry model of

Jesus found in Luke 24. In summary, a chaplain's ministry of presence can never be undervalued.

Perhaps this is why some of my own unit members often tell me that while they may forget the content of my sermons, they will never forget the times that I was *present with them* in their workplace, in a crisis-counseling situation, in a hospital room, at a funeral, and during a wartime deployment.

A Call to Prophetic Ministry
(Isaiah 6:8, Jeremiah 1:5, Philippians 1:12-14)

Isaiah 6 records the dramatic commissioning of the prophet Isaiah. After receiving cleansing and atonement for sin, Isaiah hears the voice of the Lord saying, "Whom shall I send? And who will *go* for us?" Isaiah replies, "Here am I. *Send* me!" (Isaiah 6:8, NIV, emphasis mine). Without hesitation, Isaiah steps forward with boldness to carry forth a prophetic ministry to *wherever* the Lord sends him. Likewise, Jeremiah 1 records the global nature of the prophet's call to ministry. In this case, the Lord knew Jeremiah before he was formed in his mother's womb and *set him apart* and appointed him as a prophet *to the nations* (Jeremiah 1:5, NIV, emphasis mine).

The mobile nature of military service often requires chaplains to be *sent forth* into the corners of the earth to provide ministry *wherever* there are military personnel. While providing for the free exercise of religion for military personnel, the gospel has also been carried into countries where Christian missionaries were once banned. A recent article stated, "While soldiers, sailors, and airmen are lauded each July 4th for defending freedom on a daily basis, military chaplains daily offer spiritual freedom to personnel who serve in the armed forces *domestically and abroad*. 'As chaplains, we deal in relationships,' Army Chaplain Brandon Denning said. 'I never thought God would call me to be a missionary.' But ministry to military personnel is a missionary opportunity among a distinct people group, he noted. 'The military is often a culture that is overlooked as far as missions is concerned, and yet it is one of the biggest missionary fields we've got out there,' Denning said. 'We've got soldiers who need the Lord.' "[10]

One of the first official acts of civilian clergy who become military chaplains is to swear or affirm the military oath of office.[11] The military oath is a binding document that requires obedience to the legal military orders of superior officers. In essence, military members under orders can be sent wherever the military needs them. This could mean a one-year remote tour in Korea or Iceland. As a result, like Abraham, Isaiah, Jeremiah, and Jonah, military chaplains are called to global locations where they can function within their prophetic call to ministry. God often works in and through the military assignment and deployment process. After all, God is always at work behind the scenes whether one is aware of it or not.

In the life of the Apostle Paul, God used his imprisonment to spread the gospel throughout the Roman Empire. Gary Sanders of the Military Missions Network made the following observations about God's work in and through the ministry of Paul:

> The apostle Paul, during a significant portion of his missionary career, did military missions and ministry as he was with and under the Roman military and government as a prisoner. During his fourth missionary journey, he testified, taught, and ministered to many soldiers, commanders, government officials, kings, prisoners, Jews, Gentiles, and fellow believers. His own testimony of this

time period and corresponding experience is found in Philippians 1:12-13 (NIV), where he said, *"Now I want you to know, brothers, that what has happened to me* (i.e., all his experiences while being with and under the military as a prisoner) *has really served to advance the gospel* (i.e., missions and ministry). *As a result, it has become clear throughout the whole palace guard* (i.e., military and their social networks) *and to everyone else* (i.e., others in the same setting) *that I am in chains for Christ."* Here he is speaking of military missions and ministry. In his letter to the Philippians, he was seeking to encourage them about the situation regarding his imprisonment. It is also possible that he was indirectly encouraging them about involvement in military missions and ministry (Phil. 1:14).[12]

The call to prophetic ministry involves being sent to specific people and places of God's choosing. Therefore, when military chaplains focus their attention on God's call instead of the assignment location, they will see Him accomplish His work through them.

A Call to be a Shepherd
(Matthew 9:35-38)

Military chaplains are called to become shepherds to a highly mobile flock that is culturally diverse and religiously pluralistic. Using the shepherd motif as a Biblical insight into the work of military chaplains, the Gospel of Matthew records the following account of those who came to Jesus for ministry:

> Jesus went through all the towns and villages, *teaching* in their synagogues, *preaching* the good news of the kingdom and *healing* every disease and sickness. When *He saw* the crowds, *He had compassion* on them, because they were

harassed and *helpless*, like *sheep without* a shepherd. Then He said to his disciples, 'The harvest is plentiful but the workers are few. Ask the Lord of the harvest, therefore, *to send out workers* into His harvest field.' (Matthew 9:35-38, NIV, emphasis mine)

Today, people in society in general and in the military in particular are like these lost sheep. As a result, they need shepherds to lead them. Prospective military chaplains must have compassion for the lost, harassed, and helpless souls in the military. Without a shepherd's heart that is full of compassion for the lost, chaplains can begin to stray away from their divine call to ministry and dig themselves into a pit of selfish careerism and alienation from their flock.

As they minister, chaplains need to guard themselves against apathy and disillusionment so they can remain true to their calling, convictions, and covenant with God in a pluralistic setting. Military chaplains must be authentic, lest they lose their focus and sense of calling to serve as a chaplain.

When chaplains lose their pastoral and denominational identity, it affects the entire chaplaincy and often causes service members to look "off base" for churches that will meet their spiritual needs. Chaplains who compromise their faith often get labeled as "vanilla" or "plain" from having uprooted themselves from their denominational roots. Former Air Force Chief of Chaplains, Major General William Dendinger explained the importance of maintaining a priestly identity and shepherd's heart as a military chaplain as follows:

For God and Country: Considering the Call to Military Chaplaincy

> Chaplains come from a variety of religious traditions, but there is a common ground for identity. All chaplains have some religious identity based in a religious conviction. This identity is *not* the result of doing a variety of ministries. No, we minister *because of* our specific vocation, calling, appointment, and ordination. There is a divine *calling* and a human *response* to that call which is at the core and center of any chaplain. Each chaplain needs to *nourish* that identity with frequent reflection and prayer to avoid reducing our ministry to outcomes and results only. We are motivated and appreciated in many ways in the military chaplaincy, but we must *not* make awards [and promotions] the primary source of our motivation. The ultimate rationale for our ministry must be *rooted* in our divine calling and *identity*. To live on the level of praise and appreciation only will eventually diminish our ministry. Whether we call it priestly identity, divine imprint, or a unique calling from God, chaplains must begin and end with *that* foundation or motivation.[13]

Chaplains must always be on guard for the tendency to drift away from their religious traditions and therefore spiritually wither away. As a visual reminder, the Army Chaplain Corps Regimental Crest depicts a shepherd's staff that symbolizes the pastoral ministry that Army chaplains are called to provide. On the seal of the Air Force Chaplain Corps are the words "Freedom," "Faith," and "Ministry" that form the foundation of the seal.

There are many different ways that men and women receive their call to ministry in the military chaplaincy. One survey conducted by the U.S. Army Recruiting Command indicated that nine out of ten Army Chaplains believe their divine call to serve as religious leaders in the Army is supported by the organization and its mission.

According to the survey, "a spiritual calling *and* a strong relationship with the Divine are the primary forces behind a career in ministry."[14] As chaplains reconnect with their calling, they are reminded that they are ultimately servants of God and Country.

A Call to be a Servant of God, Country, Community (Matthew 20:26-28; John 15:12-13; Philippians 2:3-7)

As military chaplains serve the members of their assigned military community, they are ultimately serving both God and Country. All military chaplains, regardless of their rank, service branch and denomination are called to be *servants* in the midst of warriors. It discredits the call to a ministry of servant hood when chaplains solely focus on their military rank over their religious insignia (cross, tablets, crescent) on their uniform.

God calls military chaplains to serve others—not to be served by others. In regard to serving others, Jesus said, "Whoever wants to become great among you *must be your servant*, and whoever wants to be first must be your slave—just as the Son of Man did not come to be served, but to serve, and to *give His life* as a ransom for many" (Matthew 20:26-28, NIV, emphasis mine). Chaplains must be willing to go into harm's way to serve those on the front lines who are facing death in a war zone.

It is a dangerous job but God has called men and women to stand in the gap for the sake of the gospel. Therefore, military chaplains must be motivated by their love for those entrusted to their care. In this regard, Jesus is the prime example of service and unselfish love when he stated, "My command is this: *Love each other* as I have loved you. Greater love has no one than this, that he *lay down his life* for his friends" (John 15:12-13, emphasis mine).

For God and Country: Considering the Call to Military Chaplaincy

Christian chaplains are called to imitate Christ in their servant approach to ministry as the Apostle Paul explained as follows: "Do nothing out of selfish ambition or vain conceit, but in humility *consider others* better than yourselves. Each of you should look not only to your own interests, but also to the interests *of others*. Your attitude should be *the same* as that of Christ Jesus: Who, being in very nature God, did not consider equality with God something to be grasped, but made Himself nothing, taking the very nature of *a servant*." (Philippians 2:3-7, emphasis mine).

As chaplains fulfill their Biblical calling in the context of the military, many will find that their ministry revolves around the following three basic functions: 1) To nurture the living, 2) To care for the wounded, and 3) To honor the dead. From the American Revolution to the present War on Terror, military chaplains have focused on these three ministry skills as they serve God and Country.[15] In my own experience, my service to God and Country as a chaplain in the Air National Guard has been the most challenging and rewarding ministry in which I have ever been involved. In explaining his ministry role to a civilian clergy member, I once heard a military chaplain state that he was a *chaplain* in general to all members in his unit, but a *pastor* in particular to the Christians within his unit. What this means is that chaplains from all faiths are to serve those of any or no faith at all. In this respect, the Code of Ethics of the National Council on Ministry to the Armed Forces provides the following guidelines:

> As a chaplain in the United States Armed Forces, I will function in a pluralistic environment with chaplains of other religious bodies to provide for ministry to all military personnel and their families entrusted to my care. I will seek to provide for pastoral care and ministry to persons of religious bodies other than my own within my area of

responsibility with the same investment of myself as I give to members of my own religious body.[16]

In the nurturing role, Rick Silveira says, "Chaplains nurture a warrior's spirituality by providing religious services for those who desire them, facilitating the spirituality of those with differing beliefs, and caring for all, regardless of their beliefs. At the heart of the chaplaincy is the free exercise of religion, including the right to hold no belief."[17]

As Chaplain Silveira further reflected on his role as a chaplain to Marines, sailors, and their families at Camp Pendleton he said, "It is clear that in an all-volunteer military, every individual who signs up comes in looking for meaning and purpose [in life]. My role is to try to understand how I can affirm that sense of calling [in life] regardless of the individual's religious beliefs."[18] As persons of faith, military chaplains have a unique, spiritual role to play as they serve in the midst of warriors. A divine calling and mission requires that chaplains be visible reminders of the Holy and abide by the tenets of their faith group and endorsers' expectations.

A Call to be a Visible Reminder of God
(Deuteronomy 20:1-4; Joshua 6:2-5; John 1:14; Philippians 2:7)

As chaplains serve as non-combatants in the midst of combatant warriors, they become a visible reminder of the invisible God. In short, it has been said that chaplains are "visible reminders of the Holy." Several Old Testament passages refer to priests accompanying armies into battle. For example, the Book of Deuteronomy records the following instructions about war:

> When you go to war against your enemies and see horses and chariots and an army greater than yours, do not be afraid of them, because the Lord your God, who brought you up out of Egypt, *will be with you*. When you are about to go into battle, *the priest* shall come forward and *address the army*. He shall say: 'Hear, O Israel, today you are going into battle against your enemies. Do not be fainthearted or afraid; do not be terrified or give way to panic before them. For the Lord your God is the one *who goes with you* to fight for you against your enemies to give you victory' (Deuteronomy 20:1-4, NIV, emphasis mine).

Another example, found in the Book of Joshua, provide details for the battle of Jericho.

> Then the Lord said to Joshua, 'See, I have delivered Jericho into your hands, along with its king and its fighting men. March around the city once with all the armed men. Do this for six days. Have *seven priests* carry trumpets of rams' horns in front of the ark. On the seventh day, march around the city seven times, *with the priests* blowing the trumpets. When you hear them sound a long blast on the trumpets, have all the people give a loud shout; then the wall of the city will collapse and the people will go up, every man straight in. (Joshua 6:2-5, NIV, emphasis mine).

These Biblical accounts provide insights into the role of priests in the military operations of ancient Israel. These passages also depict the non-combatant role of the priest as a visible reminder of God and His strength to deliver Israel from her enemies.[19] Today, chaplains still serve as a visible reminder of the One who is greater than modern day weaponry and in Whom we can place our trust (Psalm 20:7).

Another Biblical insight for military chaplaincy involves the doctrine of the incarnation. The incarnation of Jesus provides insights into using a servant-based approach as a model for military chaplaincy. The fact that God became a man and dwelt among us (John 1:14) shows how Jesus entered our world, taking on the nature of a servant (Phil. 2:7). Civilian chaplains serving in the corporate sector also see the incarnation as a Biblical image of the servant approach to ministry as a chaplain. Leaders within the growing field of corporate chaplaincy have stated the following:

> A chaplain is called to be a servant to people. The approach of Jesus that worked over two thousand years ago is an approach that will still work today. People in the workplace need people who care. They need chaplains who care enough to become servants to those around them. They need chaplains who are willing to go to extraordinary lengths to meet them at their individual point of need. That need could arise at the hospital, when their marriage faces difficulty, or when their teenager rebels. Whatever the need, people respond to those willing to serve and put the needs of others ahead of their own.[20]

The doctrine of the incarnation provides another model of ministry for chaplains as they enter the culture of the military in order to live out their faith as they serve God's people.

A Call to Provide Pastoral Care and Counseling (John 3:1-21)

A final Biblical insight involves how Jesus dealt with those seeking answers to spiritual questions. In John 3:1-21, we find that Nicodemus secretly approaches Jesus at night to discuss a spiritual matter. In the same way, military members will observe a chaplain to see if he or she is "real" and would offer them a safe place to discuss their spiritual questions. Like Nicodemus, they also will watch the chaplain and wait for the right time to make their approach, often in secret to discuss a personal crisis. The matter under discussion will often involve a spiritual solution to the crisis as hand. As a result, offering pastoral care and counseling is a key ministry of the military chaplain.

In taking the servant approach as a model of ministry, military chaplains are focused on reaching out to offer spiritual care to people located outside of the institutional church setting. Chaplains can best serve others by offering themselves as a minister of presence, care, and hope. This is much different from the standard "ministry of doing" which often focuses on the minister's ability to "fix" people or try to "solve" their problems.

> The concept of a "ministry of presence" is vital for those involved in ministering to grief stricken families. A ministry of presence is best described as watching out for those suffering a loss of any sort. The minister has to be attentive to the children and adults suffering the loss. All too often, ministers "drive by," offer some official rhetoric, verse of ritual, and then leave. Ministry of presence is about listening, waiting, respecting the silences, and, as the family (or individual) moves with the minister in that journey, to do prayer, communion, confession, rituals, etc. There are times that a person does not need us to say anything or do anything other than let them cry on our shoulders. Many people have reported how, in an attempt to fill the gap of silence, others have said things that were inappropriate or hurtful and would have been better left unspoken.[21]

After my first few years in military ministry, I came to the realization that most people only seem to want God's help when they are facing a crisis. Therefore, my primary goal is to build a long-term relationship on National Guard training weekends through purposeful visitation in various work centers, such as the back-shop maintenance areas and on the flight line. The original purpose for establishing the American military chaplaincy was to have members of the clergy *serving in the midst* of warriors facing all kinds of crisis, such as loneliness, hardship, grief, depression, suicidal thoughts, anxiety, and relationship issues. My belief is that every member of my unit is either in the midst of a crisis, or has just come out of a crisis situation, or is about to enter a crisis. If I have taken the time to establish a relationship with them, the door will be open to serve them by offering pastoral care and counseling when they face the next crisis.

Conclusion

The Bible provides many insights into the various roles of those called to military chaplaincy. Serving in the midst of warriors as a minister of God's presence, care, and hope is all about being a spiritual guidepost to a lost and hurting world in need of salvation. The vocation of military chaplaincy is a high and honorable calling from God that must be answered by those He has chosen. One chaplain summed it as follows:

> For over two hundred years, brave and dedicated civilians have been answering *two callings* to their God and to their County. From the birth of this nation, to the modern conflicts of the twenty-first century, the U.S. Army Chaplaincy has been performing its ministry of presence, in the battlefield or on the post, walking side-by-side with

Soldier's souls. The U.S. Army Chaplaincy [offers] a glorious past, a powerful present, and now more than ever, a challenging future. There are reasons to ask some hard questions. *Who will be there* to walk side-by-side with our sons and daughters, sisters and brothers, husbands, wives, the souls of our soldiers? Do we want to send our loved ones into battle, without the solace, the comfort, the spirituality, the heroism that is the United States Army Chaplaincy? The vacancies are great, the need is ever-present, the service unparalleled. It is time once again *to hear* the call. Not just hear it, but *answer it*. As the prophet Isaiah said, 'Hear am I, send me.' *Pro deo et patria*. For God and Country.[22]

With our nation presently engaged in a War on Terror, military chaplains are needed now more than ever before! I can think of no higher calling today than to serve our God and Country in the military chaplaincy. Serving others through the various Biblical ministry roles discussed in this chapter will constitute meaningful ministry for many military chaplains. When military chaplains fully understand their divine call to ministry, they can best weather the unique challenges of military life.

In the next chapter, I will examine the call to military chaplaincy with a group of fifteen seminary students who participated in a vocational discernment workshop as prospective military chaplains in the U.S. Armed Forces.

CHAPTER 4

DESIGNING A CONSIDER THE CALL CHAPLAIN WORKSHOP

Introduction

Considering the call to ministry can be a difficult process for many seminarians. In fact, John McFarland said, "Never confuse the call to be a minister with the call to be a Christian. Remember this and you will live, perhaps not with success in the eyes of the world, but definitely with love in the arms of God."[1]

While a seminary student at CIU from 1996-2000, I witnessed fellow classmates wrestle with discerning their call to ministry. Their struggle was not *if* they were called to the ministry, but *where* they were called to serve the Lord with their God-given gifts, talents, and abilities.

Whether a person is struggling with a call or already has clarity about a call, it is beneficial for them to get together with a small group of trusted friends and share their perceptions of their call. The small group provides an excellent setting in which creative interchange takes place. As each person shares about his or her call, it sparks insights among other persons in the group.

As the Spirit works in all the members of the group, each person receives greater clarity. The small group not only helps discern the gift and calling in each member, but it also offers support for ministry. As a result, the small group format provides a better setting for discernment than a one-on-one encounter because the group not only discerns but also helps engage the task.[2]

This project became a resource for students to process their call to ministry by engaging them through a small group workshop that helped them discern and demonstrate their call to serve in the military chaplaincy after graduation. When a person feels called to a specific ministry outside the traditional church setting, such as military chaplaincy, there can be a greater deal of difficulty in discerning the call of God.

To some members of the clergy, the military chaplaincy appears to be nothing more than a government-run puppet show of civil religion. Commenting on this viewpoint, Alan Wilkerson said, "Most secular institutions operate in such a way as to encourage the chaplain to fit in without anyone feeling awkward, to minimize his role as priest and prophet, and to maximize his role as pastor and lubricator."[3] Therefore, the U.S. military chaplaincy may not appear to be a valid calling for some; for others, the military chaplaincy contains one of the largest mission fields in the world!

On a personal note, I sensed that God was calling me to serve Him in the Air Force as a Chaplain Assistant during the buildup to Operation Desert Shield/Storm in 1990/1991. After enlisting in 1992, God birthed a desire in me to pursue religious studies in order to meet the educational and ecclesiastical requirements to become a military chaplain. During my ten-year journey from my initial call to ministry to my commissioning as a chaplain, there were many mentors and a unique set of circumstances that God used to confirm my call to the military chaplaincy. Having served in the Air Force Chaplain Corps for over sixteen years, I want to explore how others are finding their way into the military chaplaincy to serve God and Country.

I currently serve as a recruiting assistant for prospective military chaplains in the Air National Guard. This duty involves visiting several colleges, seminaries, and conferences each year to set up a table and talk with people interested in learning more about the part-time chaplain positions in the Air National Guard. I have an interest in better understanding the motivations and factors involved in the call to military chaplaincy. Some of the pertinent questions I explored are as follows: What attracted people to the military chaplaincy? What factors motivated people to become military chaplains? How is God calling people into this specialized ministry setting? Therefore, the act of ministry this project explored concerns my role as a military chaplain recruiter and the unique factors surrounding the call to ministry of seminary students desiring to become military chaplains.

Purpose of the Project

The purpose of this project was to examine the call to military chaplaincy among current seminary students and recent graduates of CIU. The aim of this project was to help a group of seminary students at CIU discern their call to the ministry as military chaplains. The form of this project involved designing a small group workshop for students who sensed a call to serve as military chaplains after graduation.

The Project's Goals

The research goals were directly related to the purpose of this project. The goals chosen helped students discern their call to serve as military chaplains. In addition, as a chaplain recruiter, these goals helped me understand the reasons why students wanted to become military chaplains. These two goals were measured and evaluated. The research outcomes will be summarized in the following chapter. Two goals were set forth to be accomplished in this project as follows:

<u>Goal for Seminary Students</u> (As Workshop Participants)
1. To discern and demonstrate a clear call to the military chaplaincy.

<u>Goal for the Minister</u> (As a Military Chaplain Recruiter)
1. To list and interpret the common demographic factors and vocational motivations of a group of seminary students called to serve as military chaplains.

Identifying Project Participants

In order to achieve the above purpose and goals, I contacted the CIU Seminary Dean, Dr. Junias Venugopal, in February 2008 and requested permission to conduct my D.Min. project with students by holding a small group workshop in March and April 2008 for any students interested in the military chaplaincy. CIU was an ideal place to conduct the project since there are more students enrolled this year that are preparing to serve in the military chaplaincy than ever before.

After I received permission from the dean, I sent an email to other seminary faculty members to help identify any students who wanted to participate in the "Consider the Call" workshop. The workshop was also advertised in the CIU newsletter and in a PowerPoint slide show shown during the weekly chapel announcements. The initial response came from eight current students. Later, an additional seven people heard about the workshop and indicated that they would like to participate.

Of these seven additional participants, three were alumni of CIU and currently serving as military chaplains, another two students were taking classes in Liberty University's Distance Learning Degree Program in Military Chaplaincy, and two persons were considering enrolling at CIU in the next year. A detailed breakdown of the background demographics of the participants is included in another chapter.

Project Location

The original plan was to conduct the project on campus; however, it proved difficult to secure the same conference room to use for each of the three workshop sessions. After exploring other meeting locations, an excellent facility became available at Crossover Communications USA headquarters, located across the street from the main entrance to the CIU campus.

Crossover Communications is a missionary and church planting agency founded by Dr. Bill Jones, President of CIU. After requesting use of a room to conduct the project, the staff made their training room available for each of the three workshop sessions. Not having to move to a different room on the CIU campus for each of the three workshop sessions proved extremely valuable to group cohesion.

The setup of the training room at Crossover Communications was important to creating a friendly atmosphere where participants could freely share about their own call to ministry. As a result, I deliberately set up the tables in the shape of a square so that participants could easily interact with each other during each session. Overall, the training room environment was conducive for learning and offered an excellent place to conduct the workshop.

Designing the Project

The first step in designing the project involved the creation of a Prospective Military Chaplain Survey.[4] I created the survey after reading other surveys about the call to ministry that I found in several books and dissertations. It was important that I prepared questions that would help accomplish my goal to list and interpret the common demographic factors and vocational motivations of the participants.

Once I finalized the survey on paper, I created an online version of the survey using the Question Pro web-based survey program. The use of an online survey greatly aided with automatic data compilation and tracking trends. Next, I asked several people to take the survey and provide a critique. After I finalized the survey online, I sent an email invitation with the survey link to each of the fifteen workshop participants. This initial survey served as an intake form to learn more about the background of project participants.

The next step involved designing workshop sessions that directly related to the student's goal to discern and demonstrate a clear sense of call to the military chaplaincy. In my research, I examined the ecclesiastical endorsement applications used by several denominations and faith groups. While most endorsement applications were general in nature, one religious endorsing group asked specific questions of prospective military chaplains. With permission, I adapted some of these questions for use in the workshop.[5]

While searching for other resources to help in designing a workshop about the call to ministry, I discovered a helpful manual that is used by the U.S. Army. In the spring of 2001, the U.S. Army Chaplain Corps Directorate of

Ministry Initiatives convened the Chief of Chaplains Vocations Task Force in San Antonio, Texas. One of the goals of this task force was to design discernment retreat models to support chaplains, chaplain assistants, and directors of religious education in the Army to help people answer the life shaping question, "How is God calling me to serve Him?" In the summer of 2001, the task force published their manual.[6]

This manual provided book, audio, video, and internet resources for planning a discernment retreat for youth, single adults, and couples. There were also helpful outlines for one-session, one-day, and weekend retreat models. Due to the busy schedules of the project participants, I decided to hold a three-session small group workshop called "Consider the Call: Prospective Military Chaplain Workshop."[7]

Small Group Format

In working with these students, the small group format provided an excellent environment for learning about the call to ministry and discussing the call to ministry chaplaincy. I deliberately advertised this project as a small group "workshop" because each participant needed to *work through* the subject matter as opposed to being a passive listener in a seminar or lecture-based format. The small group format chosen was also suitable for an adult learning model in an academic setting.

According to Neal McBride, there are four basic types of small groups that can lend themselves to different applications and adaptations as follows:

Designing a Consider the Call Chaplain Workshop

1. Relationship (or process) groups: The focus is on group processes to establish and nurture interpersonal relationships among the members as brothers and sisters in Christ. Groups in this category are often called "growth groups," "caring groups," "fellowship groups," "covenant groups," or something similar.

2. Content groups: The primary purpose for these groups is to learn and discuss information—usually the Word of God, but not always. Relationship is important but secondary to covering and understanding the material. Many Bible studies and discussion groups for into this category.

3. Task groups: The central focus is on doing something (a job or responsibility) together as a group, usually some ministry. The group's defined task creates the purpose for meeting. Task groups include most committees or planning groups, and even evangelism groups.

4. Need-based groups: The basic purpose is to provide support for fellow group members who have or are experiencing the same or similar need. Recovery groups, support groups, self-help groups, and group counseling are all good examples.[8]

The "Consider the Call" chaplaincy workshop that I designed was most like the content group described above but also included elements of the other types of small groups. Stating the purpose of the small group workshop gave the group intentionality and direction. The primary purpose of this workshop was to assist students in discerning a call to the military chaplaincy. As a result, the workshop included pre-session assignments in the form of specific questions that participants would answer in writing and submit prior to each small group discussion session. These questions became the focal point in each of the small group discussions over the three sessions. Also, there were background readings selected that provided an additional perspective on the subject matter.

The background readings were sent via email as an attached file along with the session questionnaires as a Microsoft Word document. I sent these emails two weeks before the workshop began. Participants printed out the articles to read and saved the session questionnaires to their hard drive so they could type out their responses within the Word document. Most participants submitted their questionnaires prior to each small group discussion session. Participants also brought a printed copy of their questionnaire responses to each small group discussion session. They were highly encouraged to keep a copy of all of their work in a notebook for further study and personal reflection.

Having their work submitted in electronic format allowed me to "cut and paste" their responses into a chart that aided in analyzing and interpreting the data. While all participants completed the initial prospective chaplain survey and three questionnaires, a few participants had schedule conflicts that prevented them from attending the small group discussion sessions. I also developed a separate tracking flow chart to help keep up with each participant's attendance and progression throughout the workshop.[9]

Conducting the Project

The participants met with me for three, one-hour small group discussion sessions on the following Wednesday afternoons: March 19, March 26, and April 9. My role was to serve as the facilitator of the discussions and encouraged participants to interact with each other on their call to ministry as a military chaplain. I obtained their permission to audio record each discussion, which helped me capture important insights to include in this project dissertation. I also kept their written responses to each session to analyze for common themes, issues, and concerns that helped me interpret the data.

Session One:
Understanding the Call to Ministry

Each session in the Consider the Call Workshop focused on a different aspect of the call to ministry and addressed matters that pertained to preparation for obtaining an ecclesiastical endorsement to serve as a military chaplain. The purpose of session one was to help participants understand the factors surrounding their call to vocational Christian ministry. The assumption was that they first sensed a call to the ministry in general, and then to the military chaplaincy in particular. The background reading assignment for session one focused on the subject of decision-making and God's will. This article, written by Roy King, a professor at CIU, provided participants with practical tools for conducting a self-assessment in order to understand their call to ministry.[10]

The questions chosen for session one directly related to the two goals originally set forth in this project. These questions allowed the participants to describe their own experience of how God's call first came to them. Other questions invited participants to describe the circumstances God used to confirm their call to enter the ministry. By taking time to answer this workshop session questionnaire, each participant had the opportunity to demonstrate a clear sense of call to ministry as a military chaplain. Participating in the small group discussion further solidified each participant's understanding of the call of God on his or her life. By wrestling with specific issues raised in the session one questionnaire and small group discussion, each participant discovered how this process helped them discern the call to ministry.

Other questions dealt with the reasons why participants were pursuing vocational Christian ministry in the first place. Another question asked participants to describe the gifts, talents, and abilities that they believe would be assets to them in the ministry. These matters dealt with the common factors and vocational motivations of those called to serve as military chaplains. These questions also provided excellent data for the goal to list and interpret such factors and motivations of seminary students.

The use of questionnaires and small group discussions is extremely helpful to discerning the call to ministry. Through personal experience, conversations with hundreds of students, and in-depth research, Alice Cullinan highlights the importance of understanding the call in the following manner:

> One difficulty we face when trying to discover whether God has called us to ministry is *understanding the questions and terms involved*. What is ministry? What is a call? Aren't all Christians called to minister? Does the call come only to those who enter vocational ministry? What exactly *is* vocational ministry? Is the call always a call to the pastorate? Does the call to ministry always mean serving on a church staff? Is a call to preach different from a call to other vocational ministries? Is a call to the mission field different from vocational calls? What about bi-vocational ministry? Does a call from God ever change?[11]

These are the ever-important questions that seminary students often wrestle with during their theological studies. In most cases, students often find themselves wrestling with these issues by themselves. However, this workshop offered a small group environment where fifteen participants could better understand their call to ministry, consider the call to military chaplaincy, and prepare to answer the call to serve as a chaplain in the U.S. Armed Forces.

Session Two:
Considering the Call to Military Chaplaincy

The purpose of the session two was to invite participants to consider the military chaplaincy as a vocation. The assumption was that participants had a desire to serve military personnel but needed to voice how serving as a military chaplain directly related to their call to ministry. The background reading assignment for session two focused on the subject of vocational theology. This article, edited by Timothy Mallard, a chaplain in the U.S. Army, provided participants with an excellent introduction to understanding vocational theology and invited them to dialogue in the small group discussion.[12]

The questions selected for session two were based on the goal of the participants to demonstrate a clear sense of call to ministry as a military chaplain. As a result, this session asked participants to describe how serving as a military chaplain related to their call to ministry. Another question gave participants an opportunity to explain any doubts or concerns they might have about serving as a military chaplain. Finally, each participant discussed the matter of spiritual, physical, and emotional preparation for ministry as a military chaplain.

This session also addressed my goal to list and interpret the common factors and vocational motivations of those called to serve as military chaplains. As a result, this session engaged participants in the area of motivations for pursuing the military chaplaincy instead of, or in addition to, another ministry role in the local church pastorate, parachurch ministry or missions. The insights and data gained from session two were compiled and evaluated in the following chapter.

Session Three:
Answering the Call to Military Chaplaincy

The purpose of the session three was to challenge the participants to answer God's call to serve as a military chaplain in one of the largest mission fields in the world. The assumption was that participants did not consider the call to serve as a military chaplain as answering a call to missionary service. The background reading assignment for session three focused on a deliberate call to missions. This article, written by Robertson McQuilkin, President Emeritus of CIU, challenged participants to understand God's redemptive plan for the world and respond to God's call to missionary service as a vocation.[13]

The questions selected for session three were based on a scenario that each participant was responding to questions asked on an application to receive an endorsement from their denomination or faith group to serve as a military chaplain. The questions chosen directly related to the goal of the participants to describe a clear sense of call to the military chaplaincy and my goal to list and interpret the common factors and motivations for serving as a military chaplain.

As a result, this session allowed participants to explain which military service branch they were called to serve and why with that particular branch. Participants also explained why they wanted to serve full-time on Active Duty or part-time in the National Guard or Reserve. Another question gave participants an opportunity to list, in order of priority, the major functions of a military chaplain. Another question allowed them to describe how serving as a military chaplain was similar to missionary service.

The participants also described the controversial issues confronting the chaplaincy today and discussed how they would respond to them. Finally, the matter of providing pastoral care from a Christian perspective in a pluralistic setting was addressed. Session three wrapped up the workshop on a high note and all participants told me they felt much more prepared in understanding the call to ministry, the uniqueness of the military chaplaincy as a vocation, and how to answer the call to military chaplaincy. Participants also completed a post-workshop evaluation survey. The results of this survey will be shared in the following chapter.

Conclusion

This project consisted of various educational methods such as survey, background readings, responding to open-ended questionnaires, small group discussion, and personal interviews. The underlying premise in this project is that God is actively at work in the world today as He continues to call people to serve as military chaplains in the U.S. Armed Forces. As a chaplain recruiter, this project helped me understand how serving as a military chaplain relates to an individual's call to ministry. While I believe that only God can call a person into the ministry, my belief is that He often uses other people and circumstances to bring the call to light.

As a military chaplain recruiter, I often find that I am watering the seeds that someone else planted. The many outcomes of this project will benefit military chaplain recruiters, denominational endorsers of military chaplains, and anyone who is considering the military chaplaincy as a vocation. Evaluating the results of Consider the Call Workshop will be addressed in the following chapter.

CHAPTER 5

RESULTS AND EVALUATION OF THE CHAPLAINCY WORKSHOP PROJECT

Introduction

From the outset, the purpose of this project was to examine the call to military chaplaincy among current seminary students and recent graduates of CIU. The aim of this project was to help a group of seminary students at CIU discern their call to the ministry as military chaplains. The form of this project involved designing a small group workshop for students who sensed a call to serve as military chaplains after graduation.

This project involved the collection of data through qualitative and quantitative research methods. The data compiled through surveys, questionnaires, small group discussions, and personal interviews directly related to the goals of this project. The goal for each student was to discern and demonstrate a clear sense of call to the military chaplaincy.

My goal as a chaplain recruiter and researcher was to list and interpret the common factors and vocational motivations of seminary students that are called to serve as military chaplains. Kathleen Cahalan offers the following project evaluation insights:

Results and Evaluation of the Chaplaincy Workshop Project

The purpose of the evaluation is a statement about its overall intent and function in relationship to the evaluation's subject and audiences. An evaluation can do one or more of the following: describe and assess the quality and effectiveness of project activities and results; determine what objectives have been met in relationship to the project goals; suggest improvements in activities and resources; understand the project's impact on constituents; and analyze the project's overall strategy.[1]

Evaluation of Goal for Students as Workshop Participants:

Discern and Demonstrate a Clear Call to the Military Chaplaincy

The goal for each student was to discern and demonstrate a clear sense of call to the military chaplaincy. To fulfill this goal, each student had the opportunity to discern and demonstrate a call to military chaplaincy as follows: 1) Participate in the Consider the Call Prospective Military Chaplain Workshop, 2) Complete a Prospective Military Chaplain Survey (see Appendix A), 3) Read selected background articles, 4) Answer three workshop session questionnaires (see Appendices C-E), 5) Participate in small group discussions, and 6) Complete a post-workshop evaluation survey (see Appendix F). In order to evaluate the results of this project I will now summarize the data collected and comment on the overall strengths, weaknesses/challenges, and changes to be made in future workshops.

The open-ended workshop questionnaires allowed students to accomplish their goal to discern and demonstrate a clear call to military chaplaincy. In their own words, students were given the freedom to describe the reasons why they were pursuing vocational Christian ministry. In response to this question one student said, "God has put the ministry of sharing the Gospel so deeply in my life that I don't want to do anything else." Another student said, "I'm pursuing ministry because since becoming a disciple of Christ, all other [types of] work pales by comparison." One other student said, "A nagging feeling is telling me I need to be doing more than what I am doing, and the only way I know to do that is to obey that call and make full-time ministry my profession and my vocation." Overall, every student described their ultimate reason for pursuing the ministry as an *obedient response* to the call of God on their life.

Students were also asked to describe the spiritual gifts and abilities that they believed would be an asset to them in the ministry. One student said, "God has given me the ability and strength to be calm and walk alongside others during times of crises." One other student said, "I believe that God has gifted me with a discerning spirit which allows me to see where people really are in their spiritual walk. I also feel that I have been blessed with a tender heart which allows me to have compassion for the lost." Another student said, "What is unique about my conversion was that I was thirty-one years old when I first believed. I spent a lot of time in the secular world and I can relate to where most guys hang out on Friday nights, what they talk about, how they talk, what they are really looking for, and how lonely they feel in a crowded bar or night club. Because of this, I believe I have the ability to relate to many kinds of people." The table below summarizes the highest number of spiritual gifts and abilities of the participants.

Table 5. Spiritual Gifts of Prospective Chaplains

Number of Prospective Military Chaplains with a Particular Spiritual Gift

Teaching (5)
Evangelism (4)
Mercy (3)
Shepherding (3)
Exhortation (2)
Wise Counsel (2)
Administration (2)
Leadership (1)
Knowledge (1)
Encouragement (1)
Discernment (1)
Service (1)
Faith (1)

Table 5. Abilities of Prospective Military Chaplains

Descriptive List of Prospective Ministry Chaplain Assets

1. Remaining strong in times of crisis
2. Caring for others by offering a listening ear
3. Having an outgoing, extroverted personality
4. Create new ways to reach different age groups
5. Understanding how young people think and act
6. Writing lyrics and singing contemporary music
7. Not afraid to be assertive and voice convictions
8. Being a people person and safe person to talk to
9. Having a tender heart and compassion for the lost
10. Can relate to the unique challenges of military life
11. Playing various instruments (drums, guitar, keyboard)
12. Understanding trials of and temptations in military life
13. Communicating God's Word to the younger generation
14. Ministering to different people, including non-religious

For God and Country: Considering the Call to Military Chaplaincy

When asked to describe their experience of how God's call to the ministry first came about, students explained the inward call they received through visions, dreams, and the inner witness of the Holy Spirit. One student said, "I was in junior high and one night I was trying to fall asleep and felt God calling me into youth ministry." Other students explained the outward call through family, friends, co-workers, and military chaplains. One student said, "I knew that the Lord wanted me in ministry, but I was running away from that. It took a gentle word of encouragement from a co-worker to tell me that I should be in youth ministry."

Another student stated, "I walked away from a high paying job, prestige, the title—everything I had feverishly worked for and I left it. I left it because I realized I had lost my soul while I was working for so much gain. I came to realize material gain is nothing if it means you lose your soul in the process." In demonstrating their call to military chaplaincy, students also described how they first experienced God's call to the ministry and shared their spiritual journey to where they are today.

When asked to describe how God confirmed their call to the ministry, students explained how particular scriptures, the wise counsel of other persons, and a unique set of circumstances and experiences helped to solidify their decision to prepare for vocational Christian ministry. For example, a student said, "After helping in my youth group for many years I felt like the ministry was a good fit. I applied to CIU for their undergrad program, and then God opened the door for the military. After being in the military and at CIU, I felt a strong confirmation that God's purpose for my life at the time was ministry. I knew because God was blessing my ministry and giving me joy from the ministry" [in the Army Chaplain Candidate

Program].

A prior-enlisted sailor and Chaplain Candidate in the U.S. Navy said, "The chaplains on the U.S.S. Enterprise confirmed my call initially. I was serving as a worship leader in the contemporary evening service. When I returned home, my [civilian] pastor said that he could clearly see that chaplaincy was a good choice for me to pursue." Another student, who is pursuing ministry in the Air National Guard said, "When I started CIU, I had no money to go there. I told God that if He wanted me here, that He would have to prepare a way. He proved Himself faithful time after time. Money in envelopes would end up in my mailbox, a job opened up at the cafeteria, and scholarships became available. The Lord reinforced that He wanted me to be in ministry each step of the way as He met my needs as I was being trained to better serve Him."

In evaluating the goal to demonstrate a clear call to ministry, I discovered the reasons why people pursue vocational Christian ministry, how they experience the call differently, and how God confirms the call through His Word, the wise counsel of other persons, and a unique set of circumstances. In examining some of the ways God calls people to the ministry, Ben Johnson discusses the following sources of God's call:

1. God often speaks through an idea that emerges in our consciousness.
2. In your external world, God often speaks to you through another person's affirmation of a gift you've been given.
3. God often speaks directly through a text in Scripture, and God always speaks in accordance with the teachings of Scripture.
4. God often calls when we come face-to-face with human pain; suffering has long been the medium of God's call.

5. God speaks to us not only through the pain of others but also through our pain.
6. Stirrings of the soul are often God's whispered beckonings.
7. The prelude to a call from God often takes the form of restlessness.
8. At times God calls in such a gentle way that the engagement feels quite natural and undramatic. Sometimes a call originates in an experience as simple as an invitation by another to share in an existing ministry.[2]

Evaluation of Goal as a Chaplain Recruiter and Researcher:

List and Interpret Common Factors and Vocational Motivations in the Call to Military Chaplaincy

My goal as a chaplain recruiter and researcher was to list and interpret the common factors and vocational motivations of seminary students who are called to serve as military chaplains. This goal was measured by the data collected on the Prospective Military Chaplain Survey, which included personal demographics and background details regarding the call to ministry. In addition, participants rated their top motivations for becoming a military chaplain. The participants' written responses to the workshop questions and personal interviews helped support and supplement the survey data. After analyzing and interpreting the data, several key themes began to surface. The raw data from the survey is compiled in Appendix B.

In order to evaluate the results of this project, it is important to understand some of the background demographics of the fifteen workshop participants. The average age of the workshop participants was thirty-three.

Results and Evaluation of the Chaplaincy Workshop Project

There were thirteen males and two females of which eleven identified their ethnic heritage as White/Euro-American, two as Hispanic, and two as Black/African-American. Of these fifteen participants, twelve were married and three were single. Regarding their number of children, six participants said they had no children, three participants had two children, three participants had three children, two participants had four children, and one participant said that he had five children.

When asked what denomination they were currently affiliated with or seeking to serve in the future, they responded as follows: seven were Southern Baptist, four were non-denominational or independent, one belonged to the Evangelical Church Alliance, one to the Pentecostal Church of God, one to the Grace Brethren denomination, and one to the Assembly of God church.

When questioned about their ministerial status, eight said they were in training as candidates for ministry, one person currently served as a youth pastor, one as a solo pastor, another person was a children's minister, one person was a teacher, one person was a new active duty Army chaplain, another was an outreach pastor and new Air Force Reserve chaplain, and one person was a chaplain at a military boarding school.

Regarding their ministerial credentials, four were working towards obtaining their credentials, four were already licensed ministers, five were ordained ministers, one was a commissioned minister, and another person was an elder.

As a chaplain recruiter, it is important to know the types of occupations that prospective chaplains have held before applying to become a military chaplain. By doing so, chaplain recruiters may discover new places and avenues to recruit for the military chaplaincy. The 2000 Standard

Occupational Classification (SOC) system is used by Federal statistical agencies to classify workers into occupational categories for the purpose of collecting, calculating, or disseminating data.

All workers are classified into one of over 820 occupations according to their occupational definition. To facilitate classification, occupations are combined to form 23 major groups, 96 minor groups, and 449 broad occupations. Each broad occupation includes detailed occupation(s) requiring similar job duties, skills, education, or experience.[3]

The table on the following page lists all of the types of non-ministry occupational experiences of the fifteen workshop participants by categorizing them into one or more of the major standard occupational classifications. In my research, the highest occupational classification among workshop participants with non-ministry experience came from those with military specific occupations followed by sales and management occupations.

Table 6. Non-Ministry Occupations of Prospective Military Chaplains

Prospective Chaplains	Standard Occupational Classification (SOC) Description of Major Occupational Groups
11	Military Specific Occupations
5	Sales and Related Occupations
4	Management Occupations
3	Transportation and Material Moving Occupations
3	Food Preparation and Serving Related Occupations
2	Business and Financial Operations Occupations
2	Computer and Mathematical Occupations
2	Life, Physical, and Social Science Occupations
2	Community and Social Services Occupations
2	Education, Training, and Library Occupations
2	Arts, Design, Entertainment, Sports, and Media Occupations
2	Protective Service Occupations
2	Building and Grounds Cleaning and Maintenance Occupations
1	Architecture and Engineering Occupations
1	Personal Care and Service Occupations
1	Office and Administrative Support Occupations
1	Construction and Extraction Occupations
1	Installation, Maintenance, and Repair Occupations
1	Production Occupations

As a chaplain recruiter, it is also important to know the educational background of prospective chaplains. By doing so, chaplain recruiters may discover new avenues to recruit prospective military chaplains in a particular academic environment. The table on the following page lists different types of academic degree concentrations of the fifteen workshop participants. Several participants held more than one undergraduate degree.

Table 7. Undergraduate Degree Concentrations of Prospective Military Chaplains

Prospective Chaplains	Undergraduate Degree Major Concentrations
5	Biblical Studies
1	Pastoral Ministries
1	Family and Church Education
1	Youth Ministry
3	General Studies
2	Cross-Cultural Studies
2	Liberal Arts
1	Political Science
1	Computer Information Science
1	History
1	Social Work
1	Criminal Justice
1	Public Service
1	English
1	Theater

In my research, the highest undergraduate degree concentrations of prospective military chaplains were students with a Bible and ministry-related degree, followed by those with General and Liberal Arts degrees. As a result, military chaplain recruiters may find more students interested in the chaplaincy at a Bible College or university where students can actually major in Biblical studies or a specific ministry field. However, as this research shows, prospective chaplains come from a wide educational background.

In his instructions to young Timothy, the older apostle, Paul, says, "Don't let anyone look down on you because you are young, but set an example for the believers in speech, in life, in love, in faith and in purity" (1 Timothy 4:12). Over the last sixteen years that I have served in the military, I have noticed an influx of younger chaplains who are graduating from seminary and immediately entering the chaplaincy in their mid-twenties as opposed to in their mid-to-late thirties.

As a chaplain recruiter, I am interested in discovering the age range at which prospective military chaplains first experience their call to the ministry. According to the fifteen workshop participants, two persons received their call between the ages of 10-15 years old, four persons between the ages of 16-21, four persons between the ages of 22-27, three persons between the ages of 28-33, and two persons between the ages of 34-40 years old.

The book of Acts records the first missionary journey of the early church as follows: While the members of the church in Antioch were worshiping the Lord and fasting, the Holy Spirit said, "Set apart for me Barnabas and Saul for the work to which I have called them" (Acts 13:2, NIV). In this passage, the call to a specific work of ministry occurs during a time of worship. As a chaplain recruiter, I want to know *where* prospective military chaplains were in their life and/or ministry preparation when God first called them.

In my research, four persons stated that it was during college, four others while in a civilian occupation, nine persons while serving in the U.S. military, three persons while attending seminary, four persons while involved in a civilian church or parachurch ministry, and one person while serving as the wife of a soldier. Participants were allowed to select more than one stage of life if it applied to them. In my research, most prospective chaplains received their call to ministry while serving in the military.

For example, one person said, "I was a young Marine stationed in Beaufort, South Carolina and a regular attendee of a local [civilian] church. One morning the preacher was preaching on something totally unrelated to vocational ministry, but I sensed God whispering in my ear, 'Preach.' I shared this with my pastor and spent time praying and fasting to discern if that was truly what He wanted." Another person said, "While serving [in the Army National Guard] the Lord used my Battalion Chaplain and some other members of my unit to steer me into the chaplaincy. I was given opportunities to lead worship services and I truly enjoyed the experience as did my fellow soldiers. I kept hearing comments from others like, 'You should think about being a chaplain.'"

The call to military chaplaincy often involves certain aspects and motivations that lead men and women to pursue this unique field of ministry. Regarding the particular aspects of the call, workshop participants explained the following characteristics involved in their call to the military chaplaincy: one person had a supernatural "burning bush" experience, two persons received a dream or vision from God about their call to the military chaplaincy, ten persons had a strong inward call, five persons experienced an outward call, one person's call came while reading a *Time* magazine article about military chaplains, one person's call involved a desire to re-enter the military after completing his initial enlistment, one person explained how he was recruited by a military chaplain who saw the military as a largely overlooked mission field, and another person explained how his friends and family had been telling him for years to become a military chaplain.

In my research, all of the fifteen prospective military chaplains were able to demonstrate a clear call from God to the military chaplaincy that was confirmed through other people and a unique set of circumstances.

Others who are considering the call to military chaplaincy have taken time to reflect on certain aspects on their call. Concerning her call to the chaplaincy, Amy Maxwell, a Chaplain Candidate in the U.S. Army stated the following in her online blog:

> A call to ministry needs more than personal conviction as evidence; it must also be confirmed by other believers and the work of the Spirit. While the previous events [in my own life] assured me personally that I'm going in the right direction, confirmation should also come from the outside. Several mature Christians have provided encouragement and confirmation. They offered these words after watching me ministering or hearing me share my passion for military ministry. When someone who knows me best says I was made to be a chaplain, those words reassure me of my call. When the Holy Spirit helps me in times of ministry and military training that too offers confirmation.[4]

Steven L. Woodford serves as Pastor of the First United Methodist Church in Vassar, Michigan and as an Air Force Reserve chaplain to the 927th Air Refueling Wing at Selfridge Air National Guard Base in Mt. Clemens, Michigan. At his denominational website, he explained his motivations for serving as a chaplain as follows:

> I am a chaplain because God has called me to be a visible reminder of the Holy in some of the most unholy and difficult situations on earth; because God has granted to me the privilege of serving our service members and bringing them God's grace and God's mercy; because, in the people of the UMC, I have the prayers and support of a loving people who are willing to share one of their pastors in this vital ministry.[5]

As a military chaplain recruiter, it is important to understand the motivations of individuals who desire to serve in the military chaplaincy. As part of the Consider the Call Workshop, all fifteen participants ranked a list of ten motivations or factors that influenced them to become a military chaplain.

The table below provides a summary of their responses with the lower number being the least important and the higher number being the most important.

Table 8. Motivational Factors that Influenced Decision to Become a Military Chaplain

(Scale Key: 1 = lowest and 10 = highest rank)

Motivational Factor	Rank
Service to God and Country	8.00
Be a visible reminder of the Holy (ministry of presence)	6.80
Fulfill the Great Commission among U.S. military personnel	6.80
Personal growth opportunities	5.93
Training opportunities that will enhance pastoral care skills	5.60
Innovative ministry environment	5.33
Real challenge of military ministry context	4.93
Incentive benefits (education, pay, healthcare, retirement)	4.33
Uphold free exercise of religion for all service members	3.67
Experience the world through travel and deployments	3.60

Results and Evaluation of the Chaplaincy Workshop Project

In 2005, the Army National Guard faced a shortage of more than 450 chaplains. However, new recruiting strategies have cut that shortage almost in half in 2008, and according to a recent report, officials anticipate it virtually closing by 2010. Chaplain (MAJ) Timothy Baer, chief of Army National Guard specialty recruiting attributed the success to a series of programs. For example, the Army National Guard encouraged chaplains to recruit their peers in the clergy who might make good chaplains, rather then leave the task solely to general-purpose recruiters, which was a first for the Guard.

Baer also explained how "chaplains are an emissary of grace in this atmosphere of war [because] many people didn't realize what a chaplain does. It's taking care of soldiers, and that resonates with people."[6]

In my own research, I asked workshop participants to list any of the five different types of persons that were most influential in their decision to become a military chaplain. The table below provides a summary of their responses and confirms recent news about the influence of current military chaplains in helping recruit new chaplains who desire to fulfill their calling to serve God and country in the military chaplaincy.

Table 9. Persons Rated Most Influential in Decision to Become to Military Chaplain

Rated Most Influential	Role of Person
9 (60%)	Military Chaplain
7 (47%)	Friend
4 (27%)	Pastor
4 (27%)	Family Member
1 (7%)	Military Chaplain Recruiter

Prior military service as an enlisted member or officer is highly desirable within the military chaplaincy. Among the workshop participants in my research, I saw a strong correlation between those who aspired to become military chaplains and those who had previously served in the military. Of the fifteen prospective military chaplains surveyed, eleven persons or 73% served in the military prior to entering seminary and four persons or 27% did not.

Of the eleven prior service members in my workshop, ten previously served in the enlisted ranks and one served as an officer. In my research, I discovered some background factors regarding the initial response to the call to military chaplaincy, and the length of prior military service before pursuing a call to the chaplaincy. Concerning the initial call to the military chaplaincy, 8 people or 53% said that they "responded immediately" to the call, while 7 people or 47% did not pursue the call immediately. Of the eleven workshop participants with prior military service, the table below shows a breakdown of the length of prior service and the particular service branch.

Table 10. Prior Military Service as Influential Factor to Become a Military Chaplain

Length of Prior Service	Prospective Chaplains	Prior Service Branch	Prospective Chaplains
1-4 years	4	Army	4
5-8 years	3	Navy	2
9-12 years	1	Air Force	2
13-16 years	3	Marines	3

In my research, I also discovered a correlation between the particular service branch and duty status that prospective chaplains desire after graduation. The table below lists these factors of the fifteen workshop participants.

Table 11. Desired Military Service Branch, Duty Status as an Influential Factor to Become a Military Chaplain

Desired Service Branch	Prospective Chaplains	Desired Duty Status	Prospective Chaplains
Army	8 (53%)	Active Duty	10 (66%)
Navy	2 (13%)	Reserve	1 (7%)
Air Force	5 (33%)	Nat'l Guard	4 (27%)

Concerning the particular military service branch that workshop participants sensed a call to serve with, one person said, "My original burden was for the Marines, but since they do not have chaplains (due to the fact that the Marines are a department of the Navy) I should have been drawn to the Navy. However, having spent nine months on an aircraft carrier near the end of my second Marine tour, I pulled a 'reverse Jonah' and tried for the Army instead. With the needs of the Army so much in the news, and after much godly counsel about my future and calling, I contacted the Army. I have every reassurance that chaplaincy is where I am definitely supposed to be; I am waiting for the future to unfold."

Another person said, "I plan to serve in the U.S. Navy on Active Duty. I have already spent a considerable amount of time in the Navy. God called me to ministry when I was in the Navy. God called me to chaplaincy when I was in the Navy. I left the Navy in order to acquire the required education with the intention of returning to the Navy as a Chaplain."

An aspiring Army Chaplain said, "I feel the need to be in the Army at this point in my life, the need is the greatest here. I desire to serve fulltime on Active Duty because I do not think that I can juggle the difficulties of the local church and the chaplaincy. I think I can devote more of my effort to the troops if I am fulltime."

Another student, who had just applied to the Army Chaplain Candidate Program said, "I want to start serving part time in the Army National Guard so that I can get a feel for military life since I've been a civilian my whole life. If there is a great sense of call to go fulltime, I will do that. However, in order to get my seminary tuition paid for through the Chaplain Candidate Program, I need to serve part-time in the Army National Guard."

The Army, Navy, and Air Force each have a Chaplain Candidate Program to use as a means for attracting qualified seminary students who wish to explore the military chaplaincy as a possible vocation after they graduate. In my experience as a chaplain recruiter, the chaplain candidate program offers seminarians the opportunity to discern God's call to ministry with the military.

In my research, Table 12 depicts the number of workshop participants who currently serve in a chaplain candidate program and the number of students who are interested in serving in the program during seminary.

Table 12a. Military Chaplain Candidate Program as an Influential Factor to Become a Military Chaplain

Currently Serving in a Military Chaplain Candidate Program	Responses of Prospective Chaplains
3 (20%)	Yes
12 (80%)	No

Table 12b. Military Chaplain Candidate Program as an Influential Factor to Become a Military Chaplain

Interested in Serving in a Military Chaplain Candidate Program	Response of Prospective Chaplains
11 (73%)	Yes
4 (27%)	No

Summary of Overall Strengths

All fifteen participants completed a Post-Workshop Effectiveness Survey (see Appendix F) in order to measure the strengths and weaknesses of the project. This project presented several challenges along the way, but offered many rewarding insights in the end. For example, this project engaged in original research that was unique to the call to ministry. When a person senses a call to ministry outside the traditional church setting, such as the military chaplaincy, there can be a greater deal of difficulty in discerning the call of God. As a result, this project met a significant need for seminary students seeking help in discerning their call to the military chaplaincy.

According to the Workshop Effectiveness Survey, 85% of the participants responded that this was the first workshop or seminar they had ever attended regarding the call to ministry. Furthermore, 93% of the participants responded that they would recommend this workshop to other seminary students who are considering the call to the military chaplaincy.

The fifteen workshop participants came from a diverse group of people preparing for the military chaplaincy in the U.S. Army, Navy, and Air Force. The diversity in age, gender, ethnicity, and denomination added value to the overall quality of the responses. Furthermore, a good mix of qualitative and quantitative research methods was employed in order to obtain key data from personal interviews and small group discussions to various surveys and questionnaires.

Among the participants, 31% said that they "strongly agree" and 62% said that they "agree" that answering the pre-session questionnaires *helped them discern* their call to serve as a military chaplain. Furthermore, 69% of the participants said that attending the small group discussion sessions was the *most helpful part* of this workshop. Finally, 69% of the participants said that "strongly agree" and 31% that they "agree" that this project helped them *better understand* their call to ministry. The complete survey results are compiled in Appendix G. Some of the weakness and challenges of this project will be discussed below.

Summary of Weaknesses and Challenges

This project was not without several challenges, which became lessons learned and opportunities for future improvement. For example, due to academic responsibilities, work, and ministry schedule conflicts, not all students could participate in all of the small group discussions. According to the Workshop Effectiveness Survey, 38% of the students said that they "strongly agree" and 55% said that they "agree" that *participating* in the small group discussion sessions helped them *demonstrate their call* to serve as a military chaplain.

However, students not present for the small group discussion were given the opportunity to individually process their questionnaire responses with me as the workshop facilitator. A possible solution would be to hold the workshop at the beginning of each semester instead during the middle when major assignments are due.

Since students had other academic assignments due during the spring semester, some were delayed in submitting their written responses to the workshop questionnaires. As a result, this delayed my ability to compile and analyze data. The intent was for each student to complete the questionnaire and submit their written responses to me *before* each small group discussion session. However, receiving late work delayed my progress in writing this dissertation as I spent much time following up with some of the workshop participants. A possible solution would be to have a two-week break between each session which would allow student more time to complete and email their written assignments to the workshop facilitator.

When asked to comment on the *least helpful* part of the workshop, 48% of the participants said "completing the Prospective Military Chaplain Survey," 7% said "answering the pre-session questionnaires," 7% said "participating in the small group discussion sessions," and 38% said "the selected background readings." A final suggestion for the Prospective Military Chaplain Survey would be to add a place for students to select their spiritual gifts from a complete list of spiritual gifts. Also, there should be a place for workshop participants to write their open-ended comments at the end of the Workshop Effectiveness Survey.

Future Directions

There are many ways that the Consider the Call: Prospective Military Chaplain Workshop can be used in the future. For example, the workshop could be offered during the first week of the spring, summer, and fall semesters through the vocational placement office of a Christian college or seminary. Local military chaplains of any service branch could be invited to participate as small group facilitators and help students discern a call the chaplaincy.

The workshop could also be adapted by any denominational endorsing agency as a self-study course for persons seeking an endorsement. In doing so, the workshop could serve as a means to help applicants discern and demonstrate a clear call to the military chaplaincy. As a result, the survey and questionnaires could also be used as part of the endorsement application process.

Part of the workshop could be adapted by military chaplain recruiters who need a resource for helping prospective chaplain candidates consider the call while they attend seminary. Sections of the prospective chaplain survey could be adapted for use as an intake form and/or online survey for aspiring chaplain candidates and chaplains. Specific data can be tracked to show emerging trends.

Consequently, this project can be adapted to meet the needs of Christian colleges and seminaries, prospective military chaplains, denominational endorsers of chaplains, and military chaplain recruiters.

Conclusion

During this project, a group of fifteen seminary students accomplished their goal to discern and demonstrate a clear call to military chaplaincy. They accomplished this goal by: 1) Participating in the Consider the Call Prospective Military Chaplain Workshop; 2) Completing a Prospective Military Chaplain Survey; 3) Reading articles about understanding the call to ministry, considering the military chaplaincy as a vocation, and answering the call to military chaplaincy; 4) Completing three workshop session questionnaires in their own words;

5) Participating in small group discussions and/or individual discussions with the workshop facilitator; and 6) Completing a workshop evaluation survey.

During this project a military chaplain recruiter who worked as a researcher accomplished his goal to list and interpret the common factors and vocational motivations of a group of fifteen seminary students called to the military chaplaincy. He accomplished his goal by designing the Consider the Call Prospective Military Chaplain Workshop which became a research tool for compiling, interpreting, and listing a wide array of tables and surveys that contain data of benefit to vocational offices of Christian colleges and seminaries, military chaplain recruiters, denominational endorsers of military chaplains, and the Chiefs of Chaplains of the Army, Navy, and Air Force. This project opens the door for future research among those preparing for military chaplaincy.

Certainly those who chose to answer the call to military chaplaincy will relate to the following words of C.T. Studd (1860-1931) who served as an English missionary in China, India, and Africa: "Some wish to live within the sound of Church or Chapel bell; I want to run a rescue shop within a yard of hell. For if Jesus Christ is God and died for me, then no sacrifice can be too great for me to make for Him."[7]

It is my hope and prayer that this project and dissertation will inspire those who sense a call to military chaplaincy to take time to reflect on their call to ministry, consider the military chaplaincy as a vocation, and answer the call to serve as a chaplain in the U.S. Armed Forces.

APPENDIX A

PROSPECTIVE MILITARY CHAPLAIN SURVEY (BLANK)

Exploring the Call to Military Chaplaincy

Thank you for your interest in the military chaplaincy. Participating in this brief survey will help you discern your call to ministry as a military chaplain. The goal of this survey is to list and interpret the common factors and vocational motivations of seminary students attending Columbia International University and Liberty University who sense a call to serve as military chaplains.

1. Age: _____

2. Gender:
___ Male
___ Female

3. Ethnicity: _____

4. Marital Status:
____ Single
____ Married

Appendix A

5. Number of Children:
___0
___1
___2
___3
___4
___5
___5+

6. Denomination: _____

7. Ministerial Status (Check one):
_____ Candidate for Ministry
_____ Supply Pastor
_____ Associate Pastor
_____ Youth Pastor
_____ Senior Pastor (with staff)
_____ Solo Pastor
_____ Other: _____

8. Ministerial Credentials (Check one):
_____ Licensed Minister
_____ Commissioned Minister
_____ Ordained Minister
_____ Elder
_____ Deacon
_____ Other: _____

9. Types of Non-Ministry Employment before Seminary:
_____

10. What was your Major for your Bachelor's Degree:
_____

For God and Country: Considering the Call to Military Chaplaincy

11. Age when first called to the ministry (in general): ____

12. Where were you in ministry preparation when you first sensed a call to become a military chaplain?
__In high school
__In college
__In seminary
__In civilian church
__Other: _____

13. My call to the military chaplaincy involved (check all that apply):
____ Burning bush experience
____ God-given dream or vision
____ Specific scripture
____ Inward call
____ Outward call

14. On a scale of 1-10 with 1 being the *lowest* and 10 being the *highest*, write the number that best represents each motivation that influenced you to become a military chaplain:

____Service to God and Country

____Uphold the free exercise of religion of all service members

____Training opportunities that will enhance pastoral care skills

____Experience the world through travel and deployments

____Be a visible reminder of the Holy (ministry of presence)

____Receive incentive benefits (education, salary, health, retire)

____Innovative ministry environment

____Fulfill the Great Commission among U.S. Military

____Personal growth opportunities

____Real challenge of military ministry context

Appendix A

15. What person(s) influenced you most to become a military chaplain (check all that apply)?
__Friend
__Pastor
__Professor
__Family Member
__Military Chaplain
__Other:_____

16. Did you respond to the call to the military chaplaincy immediately?
___Yes ___No

17. Did you serve in the military prior to entering seminary? ___Yes ___No

18. If yes, how many years of prior service?
___1-4 ___5-8 ___9-12 ___13-16

19. If yes, what was your grade? ___Enlisted ___Officer

20. If yes, what service branch?
__Army __Navy __Air Force __Marines __Coast Guard

21. If yes, what was your duty status?
___Active
___Reserve
___National Guard

22. Are you currently serving in a military Chaplain Candidate Program? ___Yes ___No

23. Would you be interested in serving in a Chaplain Candidate Program? __Yes __No

24. What service branch component do you sense God calling you to serve?
__Army
__Navy
__Air Force
__Marines
__Coast Guard

25. What military duty status are you seeking after graduation?
___Active duty (Full time)
___Reserve (Part time)
___National Guard (Part time)

26. Leaders in my denomination understand and support my calling to serve as a military chaplain:
___ Definitely
___ Most likely
___ Possibly
___ Not likely
___ Definitely not

27. Have you ever helped mentor, guide, or "recruit" someone who sensed a call to military chaplaincy?
___Yes
___No

28. Would you recommend the military chaplaincy as a vocation to a seminary student or clergy member?
___ Definitely
___ Most likely
___ Possibly
___ Not likely
___ Definitely not

Appendix A

29. How satisfied are you that your seminary training will prepare you for ministry as a military chaplain?
___ Extremely satisfied
___ Very satisfied
___ Satisfied
___ Not very satisfied
___ Dissatisfied

30. Would you be interested in taking a seminary course about military chaplaincy if offered as an elective?
___ Definitely
___ Most likely
___ Possibly
___ Not likely
___ Definitely not

APPENDIX B

PROSPECTIVE MILITARY CHAPLAIN SURVEY (RESULTS)

Exploring the Call to Military Chaplaincy

There were fifteen (15) respondents to the prospective military chaplain survey. The following is a summary of the compiled quantitative raw data collected for research.

1. Average Age of Participants: 33
Youngest was 25 years old; oldest was 44 years old.

2. What is your Gender:
13-Male (87%)
2-Female (13%)

3. Ethnic Heritage:
11-White/Euro-American (74%)
2-Hispanic (13%)
2-Black/African-American (13%)

4. Marital Status:
3-Single (20%)
12-Married (80%)

Appendix B

5. Number of Children of Participants:
6 participants had no children (40%)
3 participants had 2 children (20%)
3 participants had 3 children (20%)
2 participants had 4 children (13%)
1 participant had 5 children (7%)

6. What denomination are you affiliated with now or seeking to serve in the future?
7-Southern Baptist (46%)
4-Non-Denominational/Independent (26%)
1-Evangelical Church Alliance (7%)
1-Pentecostal Church of God (7%)
1-Assembly of God (7%)
1-Grace Brethren (7%)

7. What is your Ministerial Status?
8-Candidate for Ministry (53%)
1-Youth Pastor (7%)
1-Solo Pastor (7%)
1-Other: Children's Minister (7%)
1-Other: Active Duty Army Chaplain (7%)
1-Other: Outreach Pastor/Air Force Reserve Chaplain (7%)
1-Other: Chaplain at Military Boarding School (7%)
1-Other: Minister/Teacher (7%)

8. What are your Ministerial Credentials?
4-Working Toward Credentials (27%)
4-Licensed Minister (27%)
1-Commissioned Minister (7%)
5-Ordained Minister (32%)
1-Elder (7%)

9. Types of Non-Ministry Employment before Seminary:
U.S. Navy (2 people)
U.S. Marines (2 people)

Army National Guard
Cashier
Worked Family-Owned Business
Teacher (2 people)
Sports Coach (2 people)
Fast Food
Probation Officer
Disabled Veterans Employment Representative
Insurance Underwriter
Bartender
Engineering
Grocery Store
Window Washer
Biologist Assistant
College Student Worker
United Parcel Service
Management and Supervision
Truck Driver
Computer Network Engineer
Law Enforcement
Retail Sales (3 people)
Home Construction
Factory Worker
Senior Management
Marketing

10. What was your Major for your Bachelor's Degree and any other degrees you have:
Biblical Studies (5 people – 33%)
Pastoral Ministries
Family and Church Education
Youth Ministry
Cross-Cultural Studies (2 people – 13%)
General Studies (2 people – 13%)
Liberal Arts (2 people – 13%)
Political Science

Appendix B

Computer Information Science
History
Interdisciplinary Studies
Social Work
Criminal Justice
Public Service
English
Theater

11. Age range when first called to the ministry (in general):
2 persons during ages 10-15 (13%)
4 persons during ages 16-21 (27%)
4 persons during ages 22-27 (27%)
3 persons during ages 28-33 (20%)
2 persons during ages 34-40 (13%)

12. Where were you in life and ministry preparation when you first sensed a call to become a military chaplain? (Select any that apply)
4   In college (27%)
4   In civilian occupation (27%)
9   While serving in the U.S. Military (60%)
3   In seminary (20%)
4   In civilian church or other ministry setting (27%)
1   Other: While being a military wife (7%)

13. My call to the military chaplaincy involved (Select any that apply):
1-Supernatural "burning bush" experience (7%)
2-God-given dream or vision (13%)
10-Inward call (67%)
5-Outward call %33%)
1-Other: Reading *Time* article about military chaplains (7%)
1-Other: Reading a chaplaincy brochure, confirmation from
            Holy Spirit (7%)

1-Other: Desire to re-enter the military after completing enlistment term (7%)
1-Other: Recruited by military chaplain, see military as a mission field (7%)
1-Other: Friends and family said I should become a military chaplain (7%)

14. On a scale of 1-10 with 1 being the *lowest* and 10 being the *highest*, write the number that best represents each motivation that influenced you to become a military chaplain:

Service to God and Country	8.00
Be a visible reminder of the Holy (ministry of presence)	6.80
Fulfill Great Commission among U.S. military personnel	6.80
Personal growth opportunities	5.93
Training opportunities to enhance pastoral care skills	5.60
Innovative ministry environment	5.33
Real challenge of military ministry context	4.93
Incentive benefits (education, pay, healthcare, retirement)	4.33
Uphold free exercise of religion for all service members	3.67
Experience the world through travel and deployments	3.60

15. What person(s) influenced you most to become a military chaplain (Select any that apply)?
9-Military Chaplain (60%)
7-Friend (47%)
4-Pastor (27%)
4-Family Member (27%)
1-Other: Military Chaplain Recruiter (7%)

16. Did you respond to the call to the military chaplaincy immediately?
8-Yes (53%) 7-No (47%)

Appendix B

17. Did you serve in the military prior to entering seminary?
11-Yes (73%)
4-No (27%)

18. If yes, how many years of prior service?
_4_ 1-4 (27%)
_3_ 5-8 (20%)
_1_ 9-12 (7%)
_3_ 13-16 (20%)
_4_ N/A (Civilian 27%)

19. If yes, what was your grade?
_10_ Enlisted (67%)
_1_ Officer (7%)
_4_ N/A (Civilian – 27%)

20. If yes, what was your service branch?
_4_ Army (27%)
_2_ Navy (13%)
_2_ Air Force (13%)
_3_ Marines (20%)
_4_ N/A (Civilian – 27%)

21. If yes, what was your duty status before entering seminary?
_3_ Active (20%)
_2_ Reserve (13%)
_4_ National Guard (27%)
_2_ Discharged from Military (13%)
_4_ N/A (Civilian – 27%)

22. Are you currently serving in a military Chaplain Candidate Program?
_3_ Yes (20%)
_12_ No (80%)

23. Would you be interested in serving in a military Chaplain Candidate Program?
_11_ Yes (73%)
_4_ No (27%)

24. What service branch component do you sense God calling you to serve?
_8_ Army (53%)
_2_ Navy/Marines/Coast Guard (13%)
_5_ Air Force (33%)

25. What military duty status are you seeking after graduation?
_10_ Active duty (Full time) 66%
_1_ Reserve (Part time) 7%
_4_ National Guard (Part time) 27%

26. Leadership in my denomination understand and support my calling to serve as a military chaplain:
_13_ Definitely (86%)
_1_ Most likely (7%)
_1_ Not likely (7%)

27. Have you ever helped mentor, guide, or "recruit" someone who sensed a call to military chaplaincy?
_5_ Yes (33%)
_10_ No (67%)

28. Would you recommend the military chaplaincy as a vocation to a seminary student or clergy member?
_11_ Definitely (73%)
_3_ Most likely (20%)
_1_ Possibly (7%)

Appendix B

29. How satisfied are you that your seminary training will prepare you for ministry as a military chaplain?
 3 Extremely satisfied (20%)
 6 Very satisfied (40%)
 6 Satisfied (40%)

30. Would you be interested in taking a seminary course about military chaplaincy if offered as an elective?
 10 Definitely (67%)
 2 Most likely (13%)
 2 Possibly (13%)
 1 Not likely (7%)

APPENDIX C

Consider the Call
Prospective Military Chaplain Workshop

Session 1: Understanding the Call to Ministry

Pre-Session Assignment:

1. Complete "Prospective Military Chaplain" Survey online (Question Pro.com)

2. Read the questions below and take some time for personal reflection and prayer before answering. Type your answers directly in the Word document. Use as much space as you need and be as detailed and specific as possible.

Save the document on your computer and email copy to me. Print out a copy of your answers and bring to Session 1 for our small group discussion.

3. Complete background reading: "Hearing and Responding to God's Assignments" by Dr. Roy King.

Appendix C

Session 1 Questions:

1. Explain the reasons why you are pursuing vocational Christian ministry.

2. Describe any gifts, talents, and abilities that you believe will be an asset to you in the ministry.

3. Describe your experience of God's call to the ministry. Explain how the call first came to you and where you are today in your spiritual journey.

4. Describe how God confirmed that He wanted you to enter the ministry. Include any particular scriptures, persons, circumstances, or experiences that helped to confirm the call.

APPENDIX D

Consider the Call
Prospective Military Chaplain Workshop

Session 2: Considering the Call to Military Chaplaincy

Pre-Session Assignment:

1. Read the questions below and take some time for personal reflection and prayer before answering. Type your answers directly in the Word document. Use as much space as you need and be as detailed and specific as possible.

Save the document on your computer and email copy to me. Print out a copy of your answers and bring to Session 2 for our small group discussion.

2. Complete background reading: "Consider the Call: An Introduction to Vocational Theology and an Invitation to Dialogue" by Chaplain Timothy Mallard.

Appendix D

Session 2 Questions:

1. Describe how serving as a military chaplain directly relates to your call to ministry.

2. Explain why you are pursuing the military chaplaincy instead of (or in addition to) another ministry role such as a church pastor, parachurch ministry, missionary, or evangelist, etc.

3. Explain any doubts you have about your call and/or concerns about serving as a military chaplain.

4. Describe how you are preparing yourself spiritually, physically, and emotionally for service as a military chaplain.

APPENDIX E

Consider the Call
Prospective Military Chaplain Workshop

Session 3: Answering the Call to Military Chaplaincy

Pre-Session Assignment:

1. Read the questions below and take some time for personal reflection and prayer before answering. Type your answers directly in the Word document. Use as much space as you need and be as detailed and specific as possible.

Save the document on your computer and email copy to me. Print out a copy of your answers and bring to Session 3 for our small group discussion.

2. Complete background reading: "Who's Calling: An Exploration of Missionary Call" by Dr. Robert C. McQuilkin.

- - - - - - - - - - - - - - - - - - - -

Appendix E

Session 3 Questions:

Scenario: On your application to receive an endorsement from your denomination as a military chaplain, you must answer the following questions.

1. Which particular military service branch do you sense a call to serve with and why?

2. Do you want to serve full time (Active Duty) or part time (National Guard or Reserve) and why?

3. List, in order of priority, what you would consider the major functions of a military chaplain.

4. Describe how serving as a military chaplain is similar to missionary service.

5. Describe the controversial issues confronting the military chaplaincy today and how you would respond to them.

6. Describe your understanding of providing pastoral care from a Christian perspective in a pluralistic setting such as the military.

APPENDIX F

Survey Measuring the Effectiveness of Prospective Chaplain Workshop
(Blank)

1. The "Prospective Military Chaplain Survey" was a helpful tool in listing the influences and motivations that have led me to become a military chaplain.

___ Strongly agree
___ Agree
___ Neutral
___ Disagree
___ Strongly disagree

2. Answering the pre-session questions helped me discern my call to serve as a military chaplain.

___ Strongly agree
___ Agree
___ Neutral
___ Disagree
___ Strongly disagree

Appendix F

3. The selected background readings provided me with a better understanding of the call to ministry.
___ Strongly agree
___ Agree
___ Neutral
___ Disagree
___ Strongly disagree

4. Participating in the small group discussion sessions helped me to demonstrate my call to serve as a military chaplain.
___ Strongly agree
___ Agree
___ Neutral
___ Disagree
___ Strongly disagree

5. The <u>most</u> helpful part of this workshop was:
a. Completing the Prospective Military Chaplain Survey
b. Answering the pre-session questions
c. Participating in the small group discussion sessions
d. Selected background readings

6. The <u>least</u> helpful part of this workshop was:
a. Completing the Prospective Military Chaplain Survey
b. Answering the pre-session questions
c. Participating in the small group discussion sessions
d. Selected background readings

7. The following session was the <u>most</u> helpful to me during this workshop:
a. Session 1: Understanding the Call to Ministry
b. Session 2: Considering the Call to Military Chaplaincy
c. Session 3: Answering the Call to Military Chaplaincy

8. Participating in this project helped me better understand my call to ministry.
___ Strongly agree
___ Agree
___ Neutral
___ Disagree
___ Strongly disagree

9. Participating in this project helped prepare me to serve as a military chaplain.
___ Strongly agree
___ Agree
___ Neutral
___ Disagree
___ Strongly disagree

10. This the first workshop or seminar that I have taken on the call to ministry.
a. Yes   b. No

11. I would like to see this workshop continue with future CIU students who are interested in military chaplaincy.
___ Strongly agree
___ Agree
___ Neutral
___ Disagree
___ Strongly disagree

12. I would recommend this workshop to other seminary students who are considering military chaplaincy.
___ Strongly agree   ___ Agree   ___ Neutral
___ Disagree   ___ Strongly disagree

APPENDIX G

Survey Measuring the Effectiveness of Prospective Chaplain Workshop (Results)

There were fifteen (15) respondents to the post-workshop survey. The following is a summary of the compiled quantitative raw data collected for research.

1. The "Prospective Military Chaplain Survey" was a helpful tool in listing the influences and motivations that have led me to become a military chaplain.
38% Strongly agree
62% Agree

2. Answering the pre-session questions helped me discern my call to serve as a military chaplain.
31% Strongly agree
62% Agree
 7% Neutral

3. The selected background readings provided me with a better understanding of the call to ministry.
46% Strongly agree
47% Agree
 7% Neutral

4. Participating in the small group discussion sessions helped me to demonstrate my call to serve as a military chaplain.
38% Strongly agree
55% Agree
7% Neutral

5. The <u>most</u> helpful part of this workshop was:
24% Answering the pre-session questions
69% Participating in the small group discussion sessions
7% Selected background readings

6. The <u>least</u> helpful part of this workshop was:
48% Completing the Prospective Military Chaplain Survey
7% Answering the pre-session questions
7% Participating in the small group discussion sessions
38% Selected background readings

7. The following session was the <u>most</u> helpful to me during this workshop:
38% Session 1: Understanding the Call to Ministry
15% Session 2: Considering the Call to Military Chaplaincy
47% Session 3: Answering the Call to Military Chaplaincy

8. Participating in this project helped me better understand my call to ministry.
69% Strongly agree
31% Agree

9. Participating in this project helped prepare me to serve as a military chaplain.
38% Strongly agree
48% Agree
15% Neutral

Appendix G

10. This the first workshop or seminar that I have taken on the call to ministry.
85% Yes
15% No

11. I would like to see this workshop continue with future CIU students who are interested in military chaplaincy.
85% Strongly agree
15% Agree

12. I would recommend this workshop to other seminary students who are considering the call to military chaplaincy.
93% Strongly agree
 7% Agree

APPENDIX H

Considering the Call to Military Chaplaincy
Workshop Participation Record

Participant Name	√ Progress Checks
John Smith	___ Chaplain Survey
	___ Session 1 Questions
	___ Session 1 Discussion
	___ Session 2 Questions
	___ Session 2 Discussion
	___ Session 3 Questions
	___ Session 3 Discussion
	___ Workshop Evaluation

APPENDIX I

NORTH AMERICA & INTERNATIONAL CHAPLAINCY RESOURCE LIST

There is a plethora of information and resources available on the internet about Chaplains and the major functional areas of Chaplaincy. For example, a January 2015 Google.com search using the following words and phrases yielded these results:

chaplain	19,700,000 results
military chaplain	1,380,000 results
healthcare chaplain	564,000 results
correctional chaplain	305,000 results
corporate chaplain	544,000 results
public safety chaplain	2,010,000 results
sports chaplain	7,360,000 results
disaster relief chaplain	358,000 results
educational chaplain	1,270,000 results
community chaplain	19,700,000 results

To further refine any webpage search, it helps to include double quotation marks around a single word or phrase to restrict a search to that exact word or phrase.

For example, while a Google search for the words military chaplain (without the quotes) yielded 1,380,000 results, a search for "military chaplain" (with the quotation marks) restricted results to records only containing that exact phrase "military chaplain" with just 193,000 results. There are also ways to conduct more advanced searches by following the guidelines of your favorite internet search engine.

General Disclaimer

These Chaplaincy related resources and website links were compiled in January 2015 from several reliable sources.[1] These links are provided for the information and convenience of the reader who can decide on their usefulness for their own situation. The author and publisher have no control over material published on independent websites and take no responsibility for any content contained in the websites listed below.

It should also be noted that these links may not function at a later date as website address Uniform Resource Locators (URLs) can change at any time by the maintainer of the website. If this occurs, try and access the parent home page of the website URL and search for Chaplaincy related information. Another way to find missing data is to conduct a search by utilizing your favorite internet search engine, such as Google, Bing or Yahoo.

While this vast list contains over 325 unique websites of Chaplaincy resources and Pastoral Care related ministries, **it is not exhaustive**, especially in the area of international Chaplaincy resources. While the list could have included more resources, the author and publisher compiled the best websites based on information and resources for current Chaplains and prospective Chaplains in the major functional areas of Chaplaincy.

Appendix I

In order to maintain an updated version on this resource list, the author and publisher will release an updated version in future printed editions of this book as well as post an updated list twice a year on the following: **www.ChaplainResourceCenter.com**

If you know of a website that should be considered for inclusion on the list, please send an email with website information to: **Info@ChaplainResourceCenter.com**

The following resource list of websites are categorized by the major functional areas of Chaplaincy and should be helpful to anyone seeking to serve as Chaplain or already serving in a variety of settings. The major functional areas of Chaplaincy are listed on the following pages along with pastoral care organizations, seminary degree programs in Chaplaincy, and professional development for Chaplains, and much more. The website links are listed in alphabetical order within each functional area.

CHAPLAIN RESOURCE LIST INDEX
(BY FUNCTIONAL AREA)

1) Military Chaplaincy

2) Healthcare Chaplaincy

3) Correctional Chaplaincy

4) Corporate Chaplaincy

5) Public Safety Chaplaincy

6) Sports and Recreational Chaplaincy

7) Disaster Relief Chaplaincy

8) Educational Chaplaincy

9) Community Chaplaincy

10) Transportation, Travel, and Tourism Chaplaincy

11) Clinical Pastoral Education Programs

12) Choosing a Degree Program in Chaplaincy

13) Sources of Information for Student Financial Aid

14) Faith Group & Denominational Ecclesiastical Endorsers for Chaplaincy

15) Continuing Education for Chaplains

Appendix I

16) Professional Development for Chaplains

17) North American Professional Chaplaincy, Counseling, Pastoral Care Organizations

18) International Chaplaincy, Counseling, and Pastoral Care Organizations

19) Chaplain Ministry with Military Personnel and War Veterans

20) Free Resources for Military Chaplains

For God and Country: Considering the Call to Military Chaplaincy

1) **U.S. MILITARY CHAPLAINCY**

Military Chaplains in the U.S. Armed Forces provide military personnel and their families with religious programs through which a person may exercise their right of freedom of religion. The military depends upon all faith groups to provide theologically trained, spiritually motivated, and qualified clergy members to serve as Chaplains with Active Duty, National Guard or Reserve military forces. Volunteer Chaplains may serve with the Civil Air Patrol, State Guard, and other organizations that support Federal or State-based military operations. The following links provide more information about this functional area of Chaplaincy:

U.S. Army Chaplain Corps
(Active Duty, Reserve, Chaplain Candidate)
www.goarmy.com/chaplain.html
http://chapnet.chaplaincorps.net
www.army.mil/chaplaincorps
www.facebook.com/ArmyChaplainCorps

Army National Guard Chaplain Corps
www.nationalguard.com/chaplain

U.S. Army Chaplain Center and School
www.usachcs.army.mil/

U.S. Navy Chaplain Corps
(Active Duty, Reserve, Chaplain Candidate)
www.navy.mil/local/crb/
www.navy.com/careers/chaplain-support/chaplain.html
http://www.chaplain.navy.mil/
www.chaplaincare.navy.mil
www.facebook.com/navychaplain

Appendix I

U.S Navy Chaplain Corps (Coast Guard)
www.uscg.mil/chaplain/chapels.asp
www.uscg.mil/hq/chaplain

U.S Navy Chaplain Corps (Marine Corps)
www.hqmc.marines.mil/Agencies/ChaplainoftheMarineCorps.aspx
www.facebook.com/ChaplainoftheMarineCorps

U.S. Naval Chaplaincy Center and School
www.netc.navy.mil/centers/chaplain

U.S. Air Force Chaplain Corps
(Active Duty, Reserve, Chaplain Candidate)
www.chaplaincorps.af.mil
www.airforce.com/chaplain
www.afrc.af.mil/library/chaplain/index.asp

Air National Guard Chaplain Corps
www.goang.com/Role/Chaplain
www.youtube.com/watch?v=6jycwRvAk-c

U.S. Air Force Chaplain Corps College
www.au.af.mil/au/ecpd/afccc/

1.2) U.S. MILITARY ACADEMY CHAPELS

U.S. Military Academy West Point Chaplains
www.usma.edu/chaplain/SitePages/Home.aspx

U.S. Naval Academy Chaplains
www.usna.edu/Chaplains

U.S. Air Force Academy Chaplains
www.usafa.af.mil/units/superintendent/usafa_hc

U.S. Coast Guard Academy Chaplains
www.cga.edu/cadet.aspx?id=437

U.S. Merchant Marine Academy Chaplains
www.usmma.edu/facilities/mariners-chapel/chapel-staff

1.3) MILITARY CHAPLAIN SUPPORT ORGANIZATIONS (VOLUNTEER OPPORTUNITIES)

Civil Air Patrol Chaplain Corps (U.S. Air Force Auxiliary)
www.capmembers.com/cap_national_hq/chaplain_corps
www.gocivilairpatrol.com/cap_home/clergy
www.facebook.com/CAPchaplains

Military Chaplains Association of the USA
www.mca-usa.org

State Guard Chaplaincy
http://chaplainservices.weebly.com/state-defense-force-chaplains.html
www.sg.sc.gov/Chaplain.html
www.sgaus.org/training/chaplain.asp
www.gotxsg.com/careers.php

United States Volunteer Chaplains (Joint Services Command)
www.usvjsc-chaplaincorps.info

2) HEALTHCARE CHAPLAINCY

Healthcare Chaplains are persons called by God and trained to serve in an environment of sickness, pain, birth and death. "Holistic medicine" is a term often used to explain how persons are treated as total beings: mind, body, and spirit. They can serve in large hospitals, small medical centers, hospice, palliative care, behavioral and mental health facilities, and assisted living centers. The following links provide more information about this functional area of Chaplaincy:

2.1) HOSPITAL

Association for Clinical Pastoral Education (ACPE)
www.acpe.edu

Association of Professional Chaplains (APC)
www.professionalchaplains.org

Ethics and Bioethics
www.thehastingscenter.org

Healthcare Chaplaincy Network (HCCN)
www.healthcarechaplaincy.org

Hospital Chaplains Ministry Association
www.hcmachaplains.org

National Veterans Health Administration Chaplain Center
www.va.gov/chaplain

Pediatric Chaplains Network
www.pediatricchaplains.org

2.2) HOSPICE

Aging with Dignity
www.agingwithdignity.org

Americans for Better Care of the Dying
www.abcd-caring.org

American Hospice Foundation
www.americanhospice.org

Association for Death Education and Counseling
www.adec.org

Children's Hospice International
www.chionline.org

Hospice Association of America
www.hospicecareofamerica.com

Hospice Chaplaincy
www.hospicechaplain.com

Hospice Foundation of America
www.hospicefoundation.org

Hospice Net
www.hospicenet.org

Appendix I

International Association for Hospice/Palliative Care
www.hospicecare.com

International Fellowship of Hospice Chaplains
www.ifoc.org/ifhosc.htm

Jewish Hospice & Chaplaincy Network
www.jewishhospice.com

National Association of Catholic Chaplains (Hospice and Palliative Care)
www.nacc.org/resources/palliative.aspx

National Hospice and Palliative Care Organization
www.nhpco.org

National Hospice Organization
www.nhpco.org

National Institute for Jewish Hospice
www.nijh.org

National Prison Hospice Association
www.npha.org

2.3) MENTAL HEALTH

Associated Ministries
www.associatedministries.org/pages/MHC.htm

Episcopal Mental Illness Network
www.eminnews.org

Health Ministries Association Inc.
www.hmassoc.org

Mental Health and Chaplaincy (VA Medical Centers)
www.mirecc.va.gov/MIRECC/mentalhealthandchaplaincy/index.asp

Mental Health Chaplaincy
www.mentalhealthchaplaincy.org

Mental Health Ministries
www.mentalhealthministries.net

Mental Illness Network (United Church of Christ)
www.min-ucc.org

National Alliance for the Mentally Ill (NAMI)
www.nami.org

North American Assoc. of Christians in Social Work
www.nacsw.org

Pastoral Care Network for Social Responsibility
www.ipcnsr.org

Pathways to Promise Ministry and Mental Illness
www.pathways2promise.org

Presbyterian Serious Mental Illness Network
www.pcusa.org/phewa/psmin.htm

Trauma and Victimization
www.giftfromwithin.org

Appendix I

3) **CORRECTIONAL CHAPLAINCY**

Correctional Chaplains are specially trained clergy who administer, supervise, and perform ministry in a program of spiritual welfare and religious guidance for inmates in a correctional setting. They serve as agents of God's grace and love by caring for those who are incarcerated. The following links provide more information about this functional area of Chaplaincy:

American Catholic Correctional Chaplains Association
www.catholiccorrectionalchaplains.org

American Correctional Association
www.aca.org

American Correctional Chaplains Association
www.correctionalchaplains.org

Federal Bureau of Prisons
www.bop.gov/jobs/positions/?p=Chaplain

Good News Jail and Prison Ministry Chaplaincy
www.goodnewsjail.org

Jail Chaplaincy
www.jailchaplains.com

National Prison Hospice Association
www.npha.org

Prison Fellowship Ministries
www.prisonfellowship.org

4) CORPORATE CHAPLAINCY

Corporate Chaplains are professionally trained clergy who care for the spiritual needs of employees and their families. According to recent studies, the number of workplace Chaplains has significantly increased as businesses with a Chaplain had higher productivity and morale, reduced employee absenteeism, and an healthier employee. Corporate Chaplains can be found in a multitude of settings, from manufacturing sites and transportation companies, to law offices and banks. The following links provide more info about this functional area of Chaplaincy:

Chaplains at Work
www.chaplainsatwork.com

Corporate Chaplains of America
www.chaplain.org

Corporate Chaplaincy Consulting/Capital Chaplains
www.corpchaps.com

Frontline Chaplains
www.frontlinechaplains.org

Marketplace Chaplains USA
www.mchapusa.com

Marketplace Ministries
www.marketplaceministries.com

National Institute of Business & Industrial Chaplains
www.nibic.com

Appendix I

5) **PUBLIC SAFETY CHAPLAINCY**

Public Safety Chaplaincy consists of Chaplains serving in a variety of police and law enforcement settings, with fire departments, paramedics, and emergency medical service personnel. These Chaplains have specialized training to offer spiritual care to first-responders and those affected by crisis and trauma. The following links provide more information about this functional area of Chaplaincy:

Chaplaincy USA (Public Safety)
www.chaplaincyusa.org

Emergency Chaplains
www.echap.org

Emergency Ministries
www.emergencychaplain.org

Emergency Services Chaplains
www.emergencychaplains.org

Federation of Fire Chaplains
www.firechaplains.org

Fellowship of Christian Firefighters
www.fellowshipofchristianfirefighters.com

International Conference of Police Chaplains
www.icpc4cops.org

Police and Fire Chaplains Academy
www.policechaplaintraining.com

Public Safety Chaplaincy
www.publicsafetychaplaincy.com

Public Safety Ministries
www.publicsafetyministries.org

Appendix I

6) SPORTS & RECREATIONAL CHAPLAINCY

Sports and Recreational Chaplains are specially trained clergy who provide spiritual care to collegiate and professional athletes in a wide variety of sports and recreational venues. Chaplains may additionally provide care to the organizational workforce as well as the owners and executives of the professional organization. Recreational Chaplains can be found in national parks, campgrounds, and other outdoor settings. The following links provide more information about this functional area of Chaplaincy:

A Christian Ministry in the National Parks
www.acmnp.com

Association of Church Sports & Recreation Ministries
www.csrm.org

Athletes in Action (NFL Chaplains)
www.athletesinaction.org/pro/nfl

Chaplains Connect
www.chaplainsconnect.org

Christian Motor Sports International
www.teamrfc.org

Christian Resort Ministries (RV Park Chaplains)
www.crmintl.org/index.htm

Faith Riders Motorcycle Ministry
www.faithriders.com

Fellowship of Christian Athletes Chaplains
www.fcachaplains.org

Golden Spur Ministries (Rodeo)
www.goldenspur.org

Honor Bound Motorcycle Ministries
www.hbmm-national.org

Motor Racing Outreach (NASCAR)
www.go2mro.com
www.godandnascar.com

Motorsports Ministries
www.motorsportsministries.com

Myrtle Beach Travel Park (Campground Chaplain)
www.myrtlebeachtravelpark.com/ministry.html

North American Campground Chaplains
www.woodallscm.com

Race Track Chaplaincy of America (Horse Racing)
www.rtcanational.org

RV Churches USA Ministries
www.rvchurchesusa.org/resort-chaplains

Sports Chaplains Network
www.sportschaplains.org

Sports Chaplaincy (Australia)
www.sportschaplaincy.com.au

Appendix I

Sports Chaplaincy (United Kingdom)
www.sportschaplaincy.org.uk

Sports Outreach
www.sportsoutreach.org

7) DISASTER RELIEF CHAPLAINCY

Disaster Relief Chaplains are specially trained members of a Denominational Disaster Relief team. They are mobilized by their Denominational or Organizational Disaster Relief coordinator to provide spiritual and emotional care after a local, state, or national emergency or crisis. The following links provide more information about this functional area of Chaplaincy:

American Red Cross
(Search for Training in Local Chapters)
www.RedCross.org

Billy Graham Rapid Response Team Chaplains
www.billygraham.org/what-we-do/evangelism-outreach/rapid-response-team/chaplaincy

Christian Emergency Network
www.ChristianEmergencyNetwork.org

Disaster Chaplaincy Services
www.disasterchaplaincy.org

Disaster Response Ministries
www.drministries.net

Federal Emergency Management Agency (FEMA)
www.fema.gov/training-1
www.community.fema.gov
www.fema.gov/voluntary-faith-based-community-based-organizations

Appendix I

Int'l Critical Incident Stress Foundation (ICISF)
www.icisf.org

National Association for Victim Assistance (NOVA)
www.trynova.org

National Disaster Interfaiths Network (NDIN)
www.n-din.org

National Voluntary Organizations Active in Disaster (NVOAD)
www.nvoad.org

Southern Baptist Disaster Relief Chaplaincy/Crisis Intervention
www.namb.net/disaster-relief-chaplaincy
www.namb.net/chaplaincy-crisis-intervention

Victim Relief Chaplain Ministries
www.victimchaplain.org

8) EDUCATIONAL CHAPLAINCY

Educational Chaplains can be found in many private and public schools, institutions, colleges, and universities and provide spiritual care to a religiously diverse group of students, faculty, and staff. The following links provide more information about this functional area of Chaplaincy:

Albion College Chaplain
www.albion.edu/student-life/chaplain

Dartmouth College Chaplain
www.dartmouth.edu/~tucker/spiritual

Harvard University Chaplain
www.chaplains.harvard.edu

National Association of College and Univ. Chaplains
www.nacuc.net

National Campus Ministry Association
www.campusministry.net

Tufts University Chaplain
www.chaplaincy.tufts.edu

University of St. Thomas
www.stthomas.edu/campusministry

Yale University Chaplain
www.chaplain.yale.edu

Appendix I

9) **COMMUNITY CHAPLAINCY**

Community Chaplains answer the call to provide spiritual care in neighborhoods, parachurch ministries, homeless missions, soup kitchens, and local, state, and national groups, clubs, and associations. Community Chaplains provide spiritual care for persons in their community at large. The following links provide more information about this functional area of Chaplaincy:

American Chaplains Association
www.americanchaplainsassociation.org

American Legion Chaplains
www.legion.org/honor/chaplains

Associated Ministries
www.associatedministries.org/community-chaplaincy

Boy Scouts of America Troop Chaplains
http://bsachaplain.org
http://usscouts.org/chaplain/faiths.asp
www.scouting.org/scoutsource/Media/Relationships/ChaplainRole.aspx

Chaplains on the Way
www.chaplainsontheway.org

Community Chaplain Services
www.communitychaplainservices.org

Community Chaplaincy (FCS Urban Ministries)
www.fcsministries.org/uncategorized/guide-to-community-chaplaincy

International Alliance of Chaplain Corps
www.iaocc.org

London Community Chaplaincy (Ontario)
www.londoncommunitychaplaincy.com

Los Angeles County Community Chaplaincy
www.lacommunitychaplaincy.com

Street Chaplains
www.streetchaplain.com

Veteran of Foreign Wars (VFW) Chaplain
http://vfwchaplains.wordpress.com

Washington Community Chaplain Corps
www.wc3chaplains.org

Appendix I

10) TRANSPORTATION, TRAVEL AND TOURISM CHAPLAINCY

Transportation, Travel and Tourism Chaplains provide a unique and valuable ministry of presence by caring for the spiritual needs of workers in the shipping and transportation industry, with persons traveling through airports, working in worldwide seaports, and to vacationers on cruise ships. The following links provide more information about this growing area of Chaplaincy.

10.1) AIRPORT CHAPLAINS

Airport Chapel Program (Chicago)
www.airportchapels.org

Catholic Civil Aviation Apostolate
www.usccb.org
(Search "Airport Ministries")

International Association of Civil Aviation Chaplains
www.iacac.info

National Conference of Catholic Airport Chaplains
www.nccac.us

Sky Harbor Interfaith Chaplaincy (Phoenix)
http://skyharborchapel.org

Vatican Guidance for Catholic Aviation Chaplains
www.vatican.va
(Search "Catholic Aviation Chaplains")
http://tinyurl.com/kdbde8n

10.2) CRUISE SHIP, MARITIME, SEAPORT CHAPLAINS

Cruise Line Chaplains
www.cruiseshipjob.com/clergy.htm

Lutheran Association for Maritime Ministry
www.lammworld.org

International Christian Maritime Association (ICMA)
www.icma.as

ICMA Member Organizations (Comprehensive List)
http://icma.as/index.php/members

North American Maritime Ministry Association
www.namma.org

Professional Association of Catholic Seafarers and Maritime Ministers
www.aos-usa.org

U.S. Merchant Marine Academy (Chaplain Staff)
www.usmma.edu/facilities/mariners-chapel/chapel-staff

10.3) TRANSPORTATION CHAPLAINS

Transport for Christ
www.transportforchrist.org/chapels

Truck Stop Chaplaincy
www.fbchapnet.org/truckstopchap.html

Appendix I

Truck Stop Ministries
www.truckstopministries.org

Trucking Ministries
www.namb.net/trucking-ministries

Railroad Chaplains
www.mchapusa.com

11) CLINICAL PASTORAL EDUCATION PROGRAMS

Clinical Pastoral Education is interfaith professional education for ministry. It brings theological students and ministers of all faiths (pastors, priests, rabbis, imams and others) into supervised encounters with persons in crisis. Out of an intense involvement with persons in need, and the feedback from peers and teachers, students develop new awareness of themselves as persons and of the needs of those to whom they minister. From theological reflection on specific human situations, they gain a new understanding of ministry. Within the interdisciplinary team process of helping persons, they develop skills in interpersonal and interprofessional relationships.[2]

CPE is required to become a Board Certified Chaplain (BCC) and for employment in many of the functional areas of professional Chaplaincy. A unit of CPE is also required for many seminarians as part of their degree program. The following links provide more information about obtaining CPE units from an accredited provider:

Association for Clinical Pastoral Education (ACPE)
www.acpe.edu

Association of Professional Chaplains (APC)
www.professionalchaplains.org

Association of Professional Conservative Chaplains (APCC)
www.apcchaplains.org

Appendix I

College of Pastoral Supervision and Psychotherapy (CPSP)
www.cpsp.org

Commission on Ministry in Specialized Settings (COMISS)
www.comissnetwork.org

12) CHOOSING A DEGREE PROGRAM IN CHAPLAINCY

Since 2000, the numbers of theological schools offering courses in Chaplaincy and actual degree tracks or concentrations in Chaplaincy have grown exponentially. Using a search engine, such as Google.com can help prospective students discover the number of schools and seminaries that offer a degree in Chaplaincy. For example, Google search using the following phrases produced these results:

master of arts in chaplaincy	178,000 results
master of divinity in chaplaincy	85,300 results
doctor of ministry in chaplaincy	114,000 results
doctor of ministry in military chaplaincy	144,000 results

The first several Google pages of results included Chaplaincy degree programs from a variety of religious and theological schools from the following faith traditions: Assembly of God, Baptist, Inter/Multidenominational, Brethren Church, Independent Evangelical, Catholic, Buddhist, Pagan and Nature-Based Spirituality, Muslim, Fellowship of Grace Brethren, Pentecostal, Anglican, Presbyterian, Methodist, Jewish, Orthodox, and Reformed.

To further refine your internet search for a specific degree in Chaplaincy, include double quotation marks around a word or phrase to restrict your search to that exact word or phrase. Doing so will narrow down the number of pages in your content search. When you arrive at the website for a school, navigate to the school's home page, conduct a search for "Chaplaincy" or click on the "Academics" link to locate the Chaplaincy degree concentration.

With so many schools offering a graduate or advanced degree in Chaplaincy, where should one begin to start? There are simply too many schools to include in this resource list and choosing a school is a very personal and individual decision for each prospective Chaplain based on many factors, such as one's denomination or faith background, quality of education, cost, etc. Any prospective student should perform their own due diligence before applying to a particular school. To assist someone in choosing a seminary, consider the following ten major areas that any student should seriously consider before applying to any school that offers a degree in Chaplaincy. Thinking through these areas and the questions provided will help you make a better choice because you have taken the time to consider many of the options.

1. Theology and Doctrine

Are you in agreement with the school's Statement of Faith and Core Values? Are there any major conflicts between the Statement of Faith and Core Values of the school and your own theological beliefs or doctrine? Does the school accept a diversity of students, regardless of their denominational or theological affinity, for purposes of fellowship, encouragement, edification, and ministry? Do graduates of the school reflect the Statement of Faith and Core Values?

2. Acceptance

Will this degree program be accepted by the denomination or faith group I am seeking to be affiliated, commissioned or ordained with? Will this degree be accepted by my prospective ecclesiastical endorser for chaplaincy? Will this degree be accepted by a future employer (faith-based, public or private employer, state or federal government agency)? Does this degree program meet your personal and professional goals?

3. Accreditation

Who has accredited this school and degree program? To check on the accreditation status of the school, perform a search in the **Database of Accredited Postsecondary Institutions and Programs from the U.S. Department of Education** at the following website: **http://ope.ed.gov/accreditation**

To check if the school and degree program is accredited by the Commission on Accrediting of **The Association of Theological Schools** perform a search the following website: **www.ats.edu/member-schools**

To check if the school and degree program is accredited by the Transnational Association of Christian Colleges and Schools, see the member schools listed at: **www.tracs.org/TRACS_Members_all.html**

4. Modality

Which is better…traditional classroom, online/distance learning, blended or hybrid approaches? Schools may offer the following modes of study: traditional/face-to face/residential studies, online/distance learning studies, blended approach of traditional classroom and online studies. What is the best approach for you? What are the advantages and disadvantages of earning a degree through 100% of online study? What are the advantages and disadvantages of a traditional, residential setting or blended approach of both online and residential course work?

5. Quality of Education

Am I getting a good value for my tuition? What is the student to professor ratio? Have you spoken to anyone who has graduated with the Chaplaincy degree you are seeking? What are the academic and Chaplaincy ministry credentials of the professors teaching Chaplaincy courses? Did they ever serve as a Chaplain? Have they completed any units of Clinical Pastoral Education (CPE)? Are they certified as a Board Certified Chaplain (BCC) or Board Certified Clinical Chaplain (BCCC)? Do the professors hold membership in any professional Chaplaincy or pastoral care associations? What scholarly articles or books have Chaplaincy course faculty members published in the last ten years? What library resources are available? What do Chaplains and other ministry professionals say about the quality of education at the school you're considering?

6. Chaplaincy Specific Concentration

Some schools and seminaries claim to offer a seminary degree in Chaplaincy but have only appeared to add a few required counseling and practical ministry classes to an existing M.Div. degree and call it a Chaplaincy "track" or "concentration." These programs can be misleading because they do not contain enough Chaplain-specific learning content. Make sure you compare apples to apples when comparing a degree program in Chaplaincy. How many courses are offered in Chaplaincy specific ministry and how many courses are required to obtain a degree concentration in Chaplaincy? Have you received the course titles and course descriptions of the Chaplaincy courses? Do the Chaplaincy courses provide students with the knowledge, skills, and abilities to be a professional in one or more of the major functional areas of the Chaplaincy? Is there a requirement to complete at least one unit of Clinical

Pastoral Education as part of the degree program? What other types of Chaplaincy internship opportunities are available?

7. Cost and Affordability

How much is this degree going to cost me? Does this school accept educational benefits for U.S. Military Veterans using the G.I. Bill or Vocational Rehabilitation and Employment Program? Does this school offer any discounts for being a member of a particular denomination or faith group? Are there other tuition costs? Does the school offer on-campus housing for singles or married couples with children? Are there any on-campus employment opportunities that offer a tuition discount? What is the availability of scholarships in general and for prospective Chaplains in particular? If I need to take out a student loan, how much educational debt will I have when I graduate? How quickly will I be able to find a Chaplain or ministry position to help pay off my student loans?

8. Serving in a Supportive Place of Ministry

Is there a nearby supportive place of ministry (church, congregation, parish, parachurch ministry) that I can attend and further develop some of my Chaplaincy skill sets by teaching, preaching, counseling, offering sacraments, making hospital visit, and supporting at weddings and funerals? Do the leaders at this place of worship affirm my call to ministry in general and my call to the Chaplaincy in particular? Is there a seasoned Chaplain or minister who can mentor, support, and encourage me as I grow personally and professionally?

9. School Location and Setting

Where do you prefer to study? Do you want to study in a rural or urban setting? Is the school located near any Chaplaincy internship opportunities such as a military base, hospital or correctional facility that offers a Clinical Pastoral Education program? What are the living costs in the communities close to campus? What type of employment is available to me or my family members in the local community?

10. Seminary Community Life

What forms of academic advising and mentoring can I receive from faculty? Is there a local ministerial association that I can join and become connected with others in ministry? What kinds of spiritual, personal, and vocational formation are offered? Are there any campus programs to help support my spouse and/or children while I am a student? What kinds of services and support will the seminary provide once you've graduated? Will the friendships and ministry connections I make at this school last for many years?

13) SOURCES OF INFORMATION FOR STUDENT FINANCIAL AID

There are many sources of financial aid available to those who are willing to look for partial tuition scholarships, Chaplain loan repayment programs, military officer incentive bonuses, tuition discounts in exchange for on campus employment, and more. The following information is always subject to change, but taking time to research what's available can really help offset your total tuition costs.

13.1) U.S MILITARY CHAPLAIN CANDIDATE PROGRAM & VIDEOS

U.S. Army Chaplain Candidate Program
www.goarmy.com/chaplain/candidate-program.html
www.youtube.com/watch?v=CUgF3a9IbwI
www.youtube.com/watch?v=pQpZ23CVk1g

U.S. Army National Guard Chaplain Candidate Prog.
www.nationalguard.com/chaplain
www.youtube.com/watch?v=Qrz3xR_fYfo
www.youtube.com/watch?v=ouJMalqfrY0

U.S. Navy Chaplain Candidate Program
www.navy.com/chaplain
www.facebook.com/navychaplain
http://tinyurl.com/peftt6g
www.youtube.com/watch?v=GTs7pIqCfcw
www.youtube.com/watch?v=elATcvvuk5E

Appendix I

U.S. Air Force Chaplain Candidate Program
www.afrc.af.mil/library/chaplain/howtojoin/candidate/index.asp
www.youtube.com/watch?v=NLmThUJ-dWI
www.youtube.com/watch?v=D7P1Fz24cRw
www.youtube.com/watch?v=mTToG9LvS1U
www.youtube.com/watch?v=I4V_OI1JR6s

13.2) U.S MILITARY TUITION ASSISTANCE PROGRAM
www.military.com/education/money-for-school/tuition-assistance-ta-program-overview.html

13.3) U.S. MILITARY COLLEGE LOAN REPAYMENT PROGRAM
www.usmilitary.about.com/cs/joiningup/a/clrp.htm

13.4) SCHOLARSHIPS, GRANTS, FELLOWSHIPS AND FINANCIAL AID

Award-Winning Search for the Best Scholarships
www.scholarships360.org

Best Colleges for Financial Aid
www.bestcolleges.com/financial-aid

BrainTrack Financial Aid School Database
www.braintrack.com

Church, State, and Industry Foundation (Chaplain Candidate Scholarships)
www.chaplain-csif.org

College Scholarships Test Prep Review
www.testprepreview.com

Database of Accredited Online Schools
www.onlineschools.org

FastWeb Resource in Finding Scholarships
www.fastweb.com

FedMoney Resource on U.S. Government Grants/Student Financial Aid
www.fedmoney.org

FinAid Comprehensive Financial Aid Database
www.finaid.org

Fisher House Foundation Scholarships
www.militaryscholar.org

Fund for Theological Education (Grants/Fellowships)
www.fteleaders.org

Hispanic Scholarship Fund
www.hsf.net

Military Chaplains Association (Chaplain Candidate Scholarships)
www.mca-usa.org/scholarships

Scholarships4School.com
www.scholarships4school.com

United States Achievement Academy Scholarships
www.usaa-academy.com

Appendix I

14) FAITH GROUP & DENOMINATIONAL ECCLESIASTICAL ENDORSERS FOR CHAPLAINCY

An ecclesiastical endorsement is a legal document that states that an ordained minister is spiritually, doctrinally, educationally, and professionally qualified to represent his/her church or faith community in a specialized setting (beyond the local congregation) ministering to all in a religiously diverse context. Simply stated, an endorsement is the document that makes a "general" minister a very specialized one as a "chaplain."[3]

The best way to locate an ecclesiastical endorser is to start with your local place of worship and meet with your senior clergy leader and discuss your call to ministry as a Chaplain. If they don't know who to contact next--and many do not--ask if they know of any chaplains in the denomination or faith group to connect you with. It is very important to get connected to your local place of worship and have the long term support and nurture as you discern God's call on your life. At all costs, avoid rushing into the Chaplaincy as a lone ranger, without the support of others.

To assist with learning more about a potential endorser, the National Conference on Ministry to the Armed Forces (NCMAF) has a good list of Chaplaincy endorsers and denominational websites about Chaplaincy at the following link: **http://ncmaf.com/new-endorsers/important-links**

The Department of Defense also maintains a good list of Ecclesiastical Endorsing Agents for the U.S. Armed Forces Chaplains Board at the following link: **http://prhome.defense.gov/RFM/MPP/AFCB/Endorsements.aspx**

You can also perform a web search for your particular faith group or denomination. For example, when I Google searched "Assembly of God Chaplain Endorsement" and "Southern Baptist Chaplain Endorsement" it took me directly to their webpages that contained detailed information and an application about becoming an endorsed Chaplain. If you are part of a church, fellowship or ministry that considers themselves as Independent or Non-Denominational, you can find several results when searching "Non-Denominational Chaplain Endorsement" for prospective endorsing agencies.

For an insightful article on the topic of ecclesiastical endorsements, read the article titled "The Challenges of Endorsers and Endorsements" at the following link: **http://tinyurl.com/of79og7**

Appendix I

15) CONTINUING EDUCATION FOR CHAPLAINS

Many Chaplaincy employers require applicants to be a "Board Certified Chaplain" or "Board Certified Clinical Chaplain" *after* completing four units of CPE. In addition, an applicant for Board Certification must have work experience serving as a Chaplain in one of the major functional areas, demonstrate compliance with the Common Standards for Professional Chaplaincy, Professional Ethics, Standards of Practice, and have a mastery of a detailed list of Professional Chaplain Competencies. For more information, refer to the following websites:

Associate Certified Chaplain (ACC)
Board Certified Chaplain (BCC)
http://bcci.professionalchaplains.org

Board Certified Associate Clinical Chaplain
Board Certified Clinical Chaplain (BCCC)
www.pastoralreport.com/about.html

It is also important for Chaplains to be lifelong learners and participate in different types of continuing education opportunities that will increase the knowledge, skills, and abilities after seminary and board certification. Several organizations offer specialized training in a variety of topics through in person workshops and conferences as well as online webinars. Some of these organizations also offer annual training workshops at their membership conferences. Another source for continuing education would include special conferences offered by ecclesiastical endorsers, major faith groups, and many denominations.

The following links provide more information about continuing education opportunities for Chaplains:

American Academy of Experts in Traumatic Stress
www.aaets.org

Association of Professional Chaplains (Webinars)
www.professionalchaplains.org

Chaplain Distance Learning (Online Courses)
www.chaplaindl.org

Crisis Response Training
www.klove.com/ministry/crisisresponse

Critical Incident Stress/Traumatic Event Mgt
www.icisf.org
www.cismperspectives.com
www.homelandsecurityssi.com

Crisis Response and Trauma Care (Online and DVD)
www.lightuniversity.com

Defense Centers for Excellence (Webinars)
www.dcoe.mil

LivingWorks Education (Suicide Prevention Courses)
www.livingworks.net

Grief and Loss Training Courses
www.griefrecoverymethod.com
www.courseworkingrief.com

Appendix I

National Center for Crisis Management
www.nc-cm.org

Psychological First Aid (Online Course)
www.nctsn.org/content/psychological-first-aid

Spirituality & Practice (E-Courses)
www.spiritualityandpractice.com/ecourses

16) PROFESSIONAL DEVELOPMENT FOR CHAPLAINS

It is important for Chaplains serving in any of the functional areas of Chaplaincy to enhance the professional nature of the Chaplaincy by conducting research, writing articles and books, and presenting material at Chaplaincy workshops and conferences. The following websites provide opportunities for professional development through Chaplaincy research, journals, and magazines:

ACPE Research Network
www.acperesearch.net

Association of Professional Chaplains (Conferences)
www.professionalchaplains.org

Chaplaincy Today (1998-2012 Archives)
www.professionalchaplains.org

Curtana International Journal of the Military Chaplaincy
www.justwar101.com

Healing Ministry
www.pnpco.com/pn04000.html

International Journal of Spiritual Direction
www.sdiworld.org

Journal of Health Care Chaplaincy
www.professionalchaplains.org
www.tandfonline.com

Appendix I

Journal of Pastoral Care and Counseling
www.jpcp.org

Journal of Pastoral Theology
www.spt-jpt.org

Journal of Religion and Health
www.tandfonline.com

Journal of Religion, Spirituality & Aging
www.professionalchaplains.org
www.tandfonline.com

Military Chaplains Review (1972-1992 Achieves)
https://archive.org/details/militarychaplain45unse

PlainViews (Healthcare Chaplaincy Network)
http://plainviews.healthcarechaplaincy.org

Reflective Practice: Formation & Supervision in Ministry
http://journals.sfu.ca/rpfs/index.php/rpfs

The Military Chaplain Magazine
www.mca-usa.org

Wayne E. Oates Institute
www.oates.org

17) NORTH AMERICAN CHAPLAINCY, COUNSELING & PASTORAL CARE ORGANIZATIONS

The membership of these participating groups represents well over 10,000 members who currently serve as Chaplains, pastoral counselors, and clinical pastoral educators in specialized settings as varied as healthcare, counseling centers, prisons or the military. The complete documents and information about each of the collaborating groups can be found on the following websites:

American Association of Christian Counselors (AACC)
www.aacc.net

American Association of Pastoral Counselors (AAPC)
www.aapc.org

American Correctional Chaplains Association
www.correctionalchaplains.org

Association for Clinical Pastoral Education (ACPE)
www.acpe.edu

Association of Professional Chaplains (APC)
www.professionalchaplains.org

Buddhist Chaplain Registry & Library
www.buddhistchaplains.org

Canadian Association for Spiritual Care (CASC)
www.spiritualcare.ca

Appendix I

Canadian Association for Pastoral Practice and Education (CAPPE)
www.cappe.org

Canadian Association for Spiritual Care
www.spiritualcare.ca

Correctional Service Canada Chaplaincy Services
www.csc-scc.gc.ca

College of Pastoral Supervision & Psychotherapy
www.CPSP.org

Endorsers Conference for Veterans Affairs Chaplaincy (ECVAC)
www.ncmaf.com

Federation of Fire Chaplains
www.firechaplains.org

International Fellowship of Chaplains
www.ifoc.org

International Pastoral Care Network for Social Responsibility
www.ipcnsr.org

International Prison Chaplains Association Worldwide
www.ipcaworldwide.org

International Conference of Police Chaplains
www.icpc4cops.org

Military Chaplains Association
www.mca-usa.org

Muslim Chaplains Association
www.muslimchaplains.org

Orthodox Christian Association of Medicine, Psychology, and Religion
www.ocampr.org

National Association of Catholic Chaplains (NACC)
www.nacc.org

National Association of Jewish Chaplains (NAJC)
www.najc.org

National Association of Veterans Affairs Chaplains (NAVAC)
www.navac.net

National Chaplains Association
www.nca-hq.org

National Conference on Ministry to the Armed Forces (NCMAF)
www.ncmaf.com

The United States Army Chaplain Corps Regimental Association
www.chaplainregiment.org

18) **INTERNATIONAL CHAPLAINCY, COUNSELING & PASTORAL CARE ORGANIZATIONS**

Chaplaincy is growing in many areas outside of North America as it intersects with professional counseling and pastoral care organizations. Below are some of the websites about the presence of Chaplains in many areas of the world. If you access a website that is not in English, you can use the Google browser "Translate" feature to read the webpage contents in English.

AUSTRALIA

Australian Army Chaplaincy Journal
www.army.gov.au/Who-we-are/Corps/The-Royal-Australian-Army-Chaplains-Department/Australian-Army-Chaplaincy-Journal

Royal Australian Army Chaplains Department
www.army.gov.au/Who-we-are/Corps/The-Royal-Australian-Army-Chaplains-Department

CANADA

Canadian Association for Spiritual Care
www.spiritualcare.ca

Royal Canadian Chaplain Service
www.forces.ca/en/job/chaplain-55

UNITED KINGDOM

Association of Hospice and Palliative Care Chaplains
www.ahpcc.org.uk

British Association for Counselling & Psychotherapy
www.bacpspirituality.org.uk

College of Health Care Chaplains
www.healthcarechaplains.org

Healthcare Chaplaincy Faith and Belief Group
http://hcfbg.org.uk/

Hospital Chaplaincies Council (Church of England)
www.nhs-chaplaincy-spiritualcare.org.uk/

NHS Education for Scotland (Spiritual Care)
www.nes.scot.nhs.uk/education-and-training/by-discipline/spiritual-care.aspx

Scottish Association of Chaplains in Healthcare (SACH)
www.sach.org.uk

Workplace Chaplaincy in Scotland
www.wpcscotland.co.uk

EUROPE

European Network for Healthcare Chaplains
http://enhcc.eu

Appendix I

European Counsel on Pastoral Care & Counselling
www.ecpcc.info

Healthcare Chaplaincy in European Countries
www.enhcc.eu/members.htm

International Counsel on Pastoral Care & Counselling
www.icpcc.net

International Pastoral Care Network for Social Responsibility
www.ipcnsr-peace.org

Society for Intercultural Pastoral Care & Counselling
www.sipcc.org

Society for Pastoral Psychology
www.societyforpastoraltheology.com

GREECE

Bioethics of the Church of Greece
www.ecclesia.gr/English/holysynod/committees/bioethics/bioethics.htm

Pastoral Healthcare of the Ecumenical Patriarchate
www.pastoralhealth-ep.com

Syllogos - The Church of Greece for Hospital Chaplaincy Volunteers
www.diaconia.gr

ITALY

The Pontifical Council for Health Pastoral Care
www.vatican.va/roman_curia/pontifical_councils/hlthwork/index.htm

FINLAND

Evangelical Lutheran Church of Finland Institute for Advanced Training
www.evl.fi

FRANCE

French Association for Training and Pastoral Supervision (AFFSP)
www.supervision-pastorale-fpec.fr

GERMANY

German Society for Pastoral Psychology (DGfP)
http://pastoralpsychologie.de

HUNGARY

Hungarian Association of Pastoral Psychology
www.pasztoralpszichologia.hu/

IRELAND

Association for Clinical Pastoral Education in Ireland
http://acpeireland.com

NETHERLANDS

Association of Spiritual Caregivers in Health Care Institutions
www.vgvz.nl

NORWAY

Anglican Chaplaincy in Norway
www.osloanglicans.no

POLAND

Counselling Society and Pastoral Psychology in Poland (TPiPP)
www.tpipp.pl

SWEDEN

Church of Sweden (Health Care Chaplaincy)
www.enhcc.eu/sweden

19) CHAPLAIN MINISTRY WITH MILITARY PERSONNEL & WAR VETERANS

Chaplains who minister primarily to military personnel and war veterans are well aware of issues such as readjustment after deployment, post-traumatic stress, and moral injury. The following websites provide helpful resources in this area:

After Deployment (Defense Centers of Excellence)
http://afterdeployment.dcoe.mil

Chaplains Under Fire Documentary
www.chaplainsunderfire.com

Moral Injury: An Invisible Wound of War
www.wbur.org/series/moral-injury

National Center for PTSD
www.ptsd.va.gov

The Growth Initiative
www.growthinitiative.org/research/

Veterans History Project (Library of Congress)
www.loc.gov/vets

War on Terror: Coming Home (Six-Part Video Series)
www.providencejournal.com/topics/special-reports/home-from-war
www.youtube.com/watch?v=9usu1DSCHuA

Appendix I

20) **FREE RESOURCES FOR MILITARY CHAPLAINS**

The following list of free Chaplain resources was compiled from several reliable sources and will connect you to organizations that provide free materials primarily for military Chaplains. These links are provided for the information and convenience of the reader who can decide on their usefulness for their own situation. The author and publisher have no control over the availability of free items or the material published on independent websites and take no responsibility for any content contained in the websites listed below.

1687 Foundation
www.1687foundation.com

5 Love Languages
www.5lovelanguages.com/tools/military/

Alpha Course
www.alphausa.org

American Bible Society
www.americanbible.org/bible-ministry/armedservices/scripture-provision

Biblica (Formerly the International Bible Society)
www.biblica.com/en-us/global-initiatives/military-ministry/

Blackaby Ministries International
www.blackaby.org/sot.asp

Cadence International
www.cadence.org

Child Evangelism Fellowship
www.cefonline.com

Combat Faith
www.combatfaith.com

Cru Military (Formerly known as Military Ministry)
www.crumilitary.org

E3Resources
http://e3resources.org

Faith Comes By Hearing
www.faithcomesbyhearing.com/military/militaryoutreach

Faith Deployed (Encouragement or Military Wives)
www.faithdeployed.com/resources/

Fellowship of Fathers
www.fellowshipoffathers.com/chaplains

Guideposts Military Outreach
www.guidepostsfoundation.org/military-outreach

In Touch Ministries
www.intouch.org

Military Communities Youth Ministries
www.mcym.org

Appendix I

United States Military Chaplains Bible Society
www.militarychaplaincy.com

Military Chaplains Fellowship
www.militarychaplains.org

Military Devotional
www.militarydevotional.com

The Navigators
www.navigators.org

Operation Thank You (Cards of Encouragement)
www.operationthankyou.org

Operation We Are Here
www.operationwearehere.com/ForChaplains.html

Operation Worship (Military Bible Program)
www.operationworship.com

Prayer Stand
http://prayerstand.com

RBC Ministries (Our Daily Bread)
www.rbc.org

Saddleback Resources
www.saddlebackresources.com

So Help Me God Project
www.SoHelpMeGod.org

Soldiers' Angels
www.soldiersangels.org

Soldiers Bible Ministry
www.soldiersbibleministry.org

SLM Ministry
www.sourcelight.org/military/index.php

Strength for Service
www.strengthforservice.org

Stonecroft Ministry
www.stonecroft.org

Wives of Faith
www.wivesoffaith.org

Worship 4 Warriors
www.worshipforwarriors.com

Youth For Christ
www.yfc.net/military

NOTES

Chapter 1: Military Chaplain Recruiting as an Act of Ministry

[1] John Brinsfield, "The Origins of the Chaplaincy," March 3, 04. http://www.usachcs.army.mil/history/brief/chapter_1.htm (accessed August 18, 2008) emphasis mine.
[2] David White, ed., *Voices of Chaplaincy* (Arlington: Military Chaplains Association, 2002), 2.
[3] Stephen Mansfield, *The Faith of the American Soldier* (New York: Penguin, 2005), 79-80.
[4] Naomi Paget and Janet McCormack, *The Work of the Chaplain* (Valley Forge: Judson Press, 2006), 4.
[5] See Daniel Thompson, "The Relationship Between Mentoring and Seminarians Called Into Full-Time Vocational Ministry" (Ed.D. diss., Southern Baptist Theological Seminary, 2002), 4.
[6] Paget and McCormack, 118, emphasis mine.
[7] Bashon W. Mann, US Navy Press Release, "New Clergy Sought for the Chaplain Corps," http://findarticles.com/p/articles/mi_pnav/is_200111/ai_3553277774 (accessed February 14, 2008) emphasis mine.
[8] Matt Grills, "For God and Country," *The American Legion Magazine*, (December 2005): 27.
[9] Merwyn S. Johnson, "Whose Ministry Is It?" Due West, 1997.
[10] Alice Cullinan, *Sorting It Out* (Valley Forge: Judson Press, 1999), 16.
[11] Donald Hadley and Gerald Richards, *Ministry with the Military* (Grand Rapids: Baker, 1992), 23.
[12] Officers Christian Fellowship, "Dear Chaplain: What Advice Would You Give?" *Command* 56:6 (October 2007): 6, emphasis mine.

[13] William Noble, "In the Shadow of Death: A Theology for the Church's Military Chaplaincy," http://www.usachcs.army.mil/TACarchive/ACwinspr00/noble.htm (accessed October 1, 2007).
[14] "CIU History," http://www.ciu.edu/about/history.html (accessed August 25, 2008).
[15] A copy of the "Prospective Military Chaplain" survey can be found in Appendix A.
[16] A copy of the "Consider the Call" workshop session questionnaires can be found in Appendices C-E.

Chapter 2: Chaplain Literature Review
[1] William C. Placher, ed. *Callings* (Grand Rapids: Eerdmans, 2005).
[2] Henry Schaeffer, *The Call to Prophetic Service* (New York: Fleming H. Revell, 1926).
[3] Douglas Schuurman, *Vocation* (Grand Rapids: Eerdmans, 2004).
[4] Alice Cullinan, *Sorting It Out* (Valley Forge: Judson Press, 1999).
[5] Ben Campbell Johnson, *Hearing God's Call: Ways of Discernment for Laity and Clergy* (Grand Rapids: Eerdmans, 2002).
[6] John Creswell, *Educational Research* (Upper Saddle River: NJ, Merrill Prentice Hall, 2002).
[7] John Creswell, *Research Design* (Thousand Oaks: Sage Publications, 2003).
[8] Arlene Fink, *How to Ask Survey Questions* (Thousand Oaks: Sage Publications, 1995).
[9] Arlene Fink, *How to Conduct Surveys* (Thousand Oaks: Sage Publications, 1998).
[10] Kathleen Cahalan, *Projects That Matter* (Bethesda: The Alban Institute, 2003).
[11] Neil McBride, *How to Lead Small Groups* (Colorado Springs: Nav Press, 1990).

Notes

12 Neil McBride, *How to Have Great Small Group Meetings* (Colorado Springs: Nav Press, 1997).

13 Erin Haynes, "Military is Grappling with Shortage of Chaplains," October 16, 2007 http://abcnews.go.com/print?id=3743595 (accessed February 11, 2008).

14 Andrea Stone, "Military Copes with Shortage of Chaplains," February 5, 2008 http://www.usatoday.com/news/nation/2008-02-05-army-chaplains_N.htm (accessed February 6, 2008).

15 Doris Bergen, ed., *The Sword of the Lord: Military Chaplains for the First to the Twenty-First Century* (Notre Dame: University of Notre Dame Press, 2004).

16 Carey Cash, *A Table in the Presence* (Nashville: W Publishing, 2004) 29-40.

17 Donald Hadley and Gerald Richards, *Ministry with the Military* (Grand Rapids: Baker, 1992).

18 Stephen Mansfield, *The Faith of the American Soldier* (New York: Penguin, 2005).

19 Jim Ammerman, *Supernatural Events in the Life of an Ordinary Man* (Dallas: CFGC Publishing, 1996).

20 Naomi Paget and Janet McCormack, *The Work of the Chaplain* (Valley Forge: Judson Press, 2006).

21 Daniel Thompson, "The Relationship Between Mentoring and Seminarians Called Into Full-Time Vocational Ministry" (Ed.D. diss., Southern Baptist Theological Seminary, 2002).

22 John Womack, Sr., "What is the Call to Ministry?" (D.Min. diss., Gordon-Conwell Theological Seminary, 2001).

23 Will Ghere, "The Perceived Role of the Chaplain as Identified by Various Constituencies at Fort Stewart and Hunter Army Airfield, Georgia" (Ph.D. diss., Drew University, 1980).

24 Mack Stokes, "A Call to Service" in *Military Chaplaincy: A Study of the Participation of the United Methodist Church in the Present System of Military Chaplaincy*, Board of Higher Education and Ministry, United Methodist Church, 1979.

[25] See David Yanez, *My Military Life and the Power of God* (Houston: RevMedia, 2006); John and Bonnie Riddle. *For God and Country: Four Courageous Military Chaplains* (Uhrichsville: Barbour Publishing, 2003).

[26] See Brian Reck, *A Chaplain Experience* (Baltimore: Publish America, 2005); Patrick McLaughlin, *No Atheists in Foxholes: Prayers and Reflections from the Front* (Nashville: Thomas Nelson, 2008); William McCoy, *Under Orders: A Spiritual Handbook for Military Personnel* (Ozark: ACW Press, 2005).

[27] See Charles Grooms, *The Chaplain: Fighting the Bullets* (Raleigh: Ivy House Publishing, 2002).

[28] See David White, ed., *Voices of Chaplaincy* (Arlington: Military Chaplains Association, 2002).

Chapter 3: Biblical Insights into the Call to Military Chaplaincy

[1] Joseph Aldrich, *Life-Style Evangelism* (Portland: Multnomah Press, 1981), 19-20, emphasis mine.

[2] Rick Bereit, *In His Service: A Guide to Christian Living in the Military* (Colorado Springs: Dawson Media, 2002), xiii.

[3] Chris Lawrence, "Called to Courage," *Worldwide Challenge*, 35, no. 1 (January/February 2008): 26-27.

[4] Bereit, xiii.

[5] David Curlin, "I Will Follow Him," *CIU Connection* (Spring 2008): 13, emphasis mine.

[6] Bill Cecchini, comment on "The Number One Cause of Atheism," Friendly Christian Blog, online video posted July 15, 2008, http://friendlychristian.com/the-number-one-cause-of-atheism (accessed September 5, 2008).

[7] Paget and McCormack, 6.

[8] Monique Angle, "Chaplains See Ministering to Troops as Calling," *The State* (Columbia, SC), 26 January 2003, A8.

[9] Bergen, 221-222, emphasis mine.

[10] Keith Collier, "Chaplains Serve as Missionaries with a Military Culture," *The Baptist Standard* (July 3, 2008) http://www.baptiststandard.com (accessed September 5, 2008).

[11] See Brian Bohlman, *So Help Me God: A Reflection on the Military Oath* (Columbia: So Help Me God Project, 2005).

[12] Gary Sanders, "Military Missions," http://www.militarymissionsnetwork.com. (accessed September 5, 2008).

[13] White, 40, emphasis mine.

[14] United States Army, "U.S. Army Chaplains Report High Job Fulfillment," http://www.goarmy.com/chaplain/news_detail.jsp?article=story13 (accessed April 27, 2007).

[15] James Spivey, "From Our National President," *The Military Chaplain* 80, no. 1 (March 2007): 3.

[16] National Council on Ministry to the Armed Forces, "Code of Ethics for Chaplains in the Armed Forces," http://www.ncmaf.org/policies/codeofethics.htm (accessed April 25, 2007).

[17] Ellen Woods, "Higher Calling," *Military Officer*, September 2006: 103.

[18] Ibid, 104.

[19] See Exodus 17: 8-16 for the priestly role of Aaron and Hur in supporting Moses during war.

[20] Mark Cress, Chris Hobgood, and Dwayne Reece, *The Complete Corporate Chaplain's Handbook* (Wake Forest: Lanphier Press, 2006), 41.

[21] Cress, 213.

[22] Kenneth Beale, *For God and Country: U.S. Army Chaplain Recruiting* (Fort Knox, KY: 2005), DVD, emphasis mine.

Chapter 4: Designing a Consider the Call Chaplain Workshop

[1] John McFarland, "On Hearing the Call," *Christian Ministry* Vol. 16, No. 4 (July 1985): 26.

[2] Johnson, 92.
[3] Alan Wilkerson, "The Paradox of the Military Chaplain," *Theology* Vol 84 (July 1981): 250.
[4] A copy of the "Prospective Military Chaplain" survey can be found in Appendix A.
[5] The Coalition of Spirit-filled Churches, Application for Ecclesiastical Endorsement, http://www.spirit-filled.org (accessed February 6, 2008).
[6] Timothy S. Mallard, ed., "Consider The Call: A Vocations Resource Manual (From a Christian Faith Perspective)," Washington, D.C., 2001.
[7] A copy of the "Consider the Call" workshop questionnaires can be found in Appendices C-E.
[8] Neal McBride, *How to Have Great Small Group Meetings* (Colorado Springs: NavPress, 1997) 14-15.
[9] A copy of the "Workshop Participation Record" can be found in Appendix H.
[10] Roy King, "Hearing and Responding to God's Assignments" (Columbia, 2006).
[11] Cullinan, 2, emphasis mine.
[12] Mallard, 10-19.
[13] Robertson McQuilkin, "Who's Calling? An Exploration of the Missionary Call" (Columbia, 1984).

Chapter 5: Results and Evaluation of the Project
[1] Kathleen A. Cahalan, *Projects That Matter* (Bethesda: The Alban Institute, 2003), 37.
[2] Johnson, 36-44.
[3] U.S. Department of Labor, http://www.bls.gov/soc/ (accessed July 28, 2008).
[4] Amy Maxwell, comment on "My Call to the Military," Gentle Whisper Blog, comment posted May 2, 2008, http://gentlewhisper.com/blog/2008/05/02/my-call (accessed July 28, 2008).
[5] Steven L. Woodford, "Why I'm a Chaplain,"

http://www.gbhem.org/chaplains/Stories.asp?action=&id=102 (accessed January 10, 2007).
[6] Jim Greenhill, "Army Guard Reduces Shortage of Chaplains," *National Guard* Vol. 62 No. 7 (July 2008) 19.
[7] C.T. Studd, Missionary Biographies, http://www.wholesomewords.org/missions/istudd.html (accessed August 13, 2008).

Appendix I: Chaplaincy Related Resource List

[1] The idea to compile a new list of Chaplaincy websites in the major functional areas of Chaplaincy came after reading "Chaplaincy: The Greatest Story Never Told," by Rev. David Plummer in *The Journal of Pastoral Care* 50 (1996): 1-11. In order to prepare and expand upon his idea, the following websites were accessed in January 2015 to compile a detailed listings of chaplaincy related resources in the major functional areas of Chaplaincy: www.ProfessionalChaplains.org; www.Spirit-Filled.org; www.TheNewCenturion.com. Another source consulted was the appendix section by Joel Graves in *Leadership Paradigms in Chaplaincy* (Dissertation.com, 2007).
[2] See "What is Clinical Pastoral Education" article at http://s531162813.onlinehome.us/faq/ (Accessed 7 Jan 15)
[3] See article at www.spirit-filled.org/endorsement.html for a good overview about what a Chaplaincy endorsement really is and is not. (Accessed 7 Jan 15)

BIBLIOGRAPHY

Aldrich, Joseph. *Life-Style Evangelism*. Portland: Multnomah Press, 1981.

Angle, Monique. "Chaplains See Ministering to Troops as Calling." *The State*, Final Edition, January 26, 2003, A-8.

Ammerman, Jim. *Supernatural Events in the Life of an Ordinary Man*. Dallas: CFGC Press, 1996.

Baxter, Richard. *The Reformed Pastor*. Grand Rapids: Sovereign Grace Publishers, 1971.

Bereit, Rick. *In His Service: A Guide to Christian Living in the Military*. Colorado Springs: Dawson Media, 2002.

Bergen, Doris, ed. *The Sword of the Lord*. Notre Dame: University of Notre Dame Press, 2004.

Bohlman, Brian. *So Help Me God: A Reflection on the Military Oath*. Columbia: So Help Me God Project, 2005.

Cahalan, Kathleen. *Projects That Matter*. Bethesda: The Alban Institute, 2003.

Cash, Carey. *A Table in the Presence*. Nashville: W Publishing, 2004.

Clowney, Edmund. *Called to the Ministry*. Phillipsburg, NJ: P & R Publishing, 1976.

Collier, Keith. "Chaplains Serve as Missionaries With a Military Culture." *The Baptist Standard* (July 3, 2008) http://www.baptiststandard.com (accessed September 5, 2008).

Bibliography

Creswell, John. *Educational Research*. Upper Saddle River: NJ, Merrill Prentice Hall, 2002.

_____. *Research Design*. Thousand Oaks: Sage Publications, 2003.

Cress, Mark., Chris Hobgood, and Dwayne Reece, *The Complete Corporate Chaplain's Handbook,* rev. ed., Wake Forest: Lanphier Press, 2006.

Cullinan, Alice. *Sorting It Out*. Valley Forge: Judson Press, 1999.

Curlin, David. "I Will Follow Him," *CIU Connection,* Spring 2008, 13.

Fink, Arlene. *How to Ask Survey Questions*. Thousand Oaks: Sage Publications, 1995.

_____. *How to Conduct Surveys*. Thousand Oaks: Sage Publications, 1998.

Friendly Christian Blog. http://www.friendlychristian.com (accessed September 5, 2008).

Ghere, Will. "The Perceived Role of the Chaplain as Identified by Various Constituencies at Fort Stewart and Hunter Army Airfield, Georgia." Ph.D. diss., Drew University, 1980.

Greenhill, Jim. "Army Guard Reduces Shortage of Chaplains," *National Guard* Vol. 62, No. 7 (July 2008): 19.

Grills, Matt. "For God and Country," *The American Legion Magazine*, December 2005, 27.

Grooms, Charles. *The Chaplain: Fighting the Bullets*. Raleigh: Ivy House, 2002.

Hadley, Donald and Gerald Richards. *Ministry with the Military: A Guide for Churches and Chaplains*. Grand Rapids: Baker, 1992.

Haynes, Erin. "Military is Grappling with Shortage of Chaplains," (October 16, 2007) http://abcnews.go.com/print?id=3743595 (accessed February 11, 2008).

Lawrence, Chris. "Called to Courage," *Worldwide Challenge*, Vol 35, No 1 (January/February 2008): 26-27.

Johnson, Ben Campbell. *Hearing God's Call: Ways of Discernment for Laity and Clergy*. Grand Rapids: Eerdmans Publishing, 2002.

Johnson, Joseph. "Revisioning the Inward Call to Ministry: A Practical Theological Analysis of Second-Career Methodist Seminarians." Ph.D. diss., Vanderbilt University, 1980.

Johnson, Merwyn. "Whose Ministry is it?" Lecture on the Issue of Instrumentality and the Theology of Ministry, Erskine Theological Seminary, Due West, SC, August 1997.

King, Roy. "Hearing and Responding to God's Assignments." Columbia International University, 2006.

Mallard, Timothy.,ed., "Consider The Call: A Vocations Resource Manual (From a Christian Faith Perspective)." Washington, D.C., 2001.

Bibliography

Mann, Bashon W. US Navy Press Release, "New Clergy Sought for the Chaplain Corps," http://findarticles.com/p/articles/mi_pnav/is_200111/ai_3553277774 (accessed February 14, 2008).

Mansfield, Stephen. *The Faith of the American Soldier*. New York: Penguin, 2005.

Maxwell, Amy. Comment on "My Call to the Military," Gentle Whisper Blog, comment posted May 2, 2008, http://gentlewhisper.com/blog/2008/05/02/my-call (accessed July 28, 2008).

McBride, Neil. *How to Lead Small Groups*. Colorado Springs: Nav Press, 1990.

_____. *How to Have Great Small Group Meetings*. Colorado Springs: Nav Press, 1997.

McCoy, William. *Under Orders: A Spiritual Handbook for Military Personnel*. Ozark: ACW Press, 2005.

McFarland, John R. "On Hearing the Call." *Christian Ministry*, Vol 16, No. 4 (July 1985): 25-26.

McLaughlin, Patrick. *No Atheists in Foxholes: Prayers and Reflections from the Front* Nashville: Thomas Nelson, 2008.

McQuilkin, Robertson. "Who's Calling? An Exploration of the Missionary Call." Columbia International University, 1984.

National Council on Ministry to the Armed Forces, "Code of Ethics for Chaplains in the Armed Forces." http://www.ncmaf.org/policies/codeofethics.htm (accessed April 25, 2007).

National Council on Ministry in the Armed Forces, "Covenant for Chaplains in the Armed Forces." http://www.ncmaf.org/policies/codeofethics.htm (accessed April 25, 2007).

Noble, William. "In the Shadow of Death: A Theology for the Church's Military Chaplaincy," http://www.usachcs.army.mil/TACarchive/ACwinspr00/noble.htm (accessed October 1, 2007).

Officers Christian Fellowship, "Dear Chaplain: What Advice Would You Give" *Command* (October 2007) Vol 56, No 6, 6.

Paget, Naomi and Janet McCormack, *The Work of the Chaplain*. Valley Forge: Judson Press, 2006.

Placher, William C. ed., *Callings*. Grand Rapids: Eerdmans Publishing, 2005.

Prawdzik, Christopher. "Soul Soothers." *National Guard*, Vol. 58, No. 1 (January 2004): 20.

Reck, Brian. *A Chaplain Experience*. Baltimore: Publish America, 2005.

Riddle, John and Bonnie. *For God and Country: Four Courageous Military Chaplains*. Uhrichsville: Barbour Publishing, 2003.

Sanders, Gary. "Military Missions Network Premise" http://www.militarymissionsnetwork.com (accessed September 5, 2008).

Schuurman, Douglas. *Vocation: Discerning Our Callings in Life*. Grand Rapids: Eerdmans Publishing, 2004.

Spivey, James. "From Our National President," *The Military Chaplain* Vol. 80, No. 1 March 2007.

Bibliography

Stokes, Mack. "A Call to Service" in *Military Chaplaincy: A Study of the Participation of the United Methodist Church in the Present System of Military Chaplaincy*. Board of Higher Education and Ministry United Methodist Church, 1979.

Stone, Andrea. "Military Copes with Shortage of Chaplains," (February 5, 2008) http://www.usatoday.com/news/nation/2008-02-05-army-chaplains_N.htm (accessed February 6, 2008).

The Holy Bible, New International Version. Grand Rapids: Zondervan, 1984.

Thompson, Daniel. "The Relationship Between Mentoring and Seminarians Called Into Full-Time Vocational Ministry." Ph.D. diss., Southern Baptist Theological Seminary, 2002.

U.S. Army, "U.S. Army Chaplains Report High Job Fulfillment." http://www.goarmy.com/chaplain/news_detail.jsp?article=story13 (accessed April 27, 2007).

White, David. ed. *Voices of Chaplaincy*. Arlington: Military Chaplains Association, 2002.

Wilkinson, Alan. "The Paradox of the Military Chaplain." *Theology*, Vol 84 (July 1981): 249-257.

Woodford, Steven. "Why I'm a Chaplain," http://www.gbhem.org/chaplains/Stories.asp?action=&id=102 (accessed Jan 10, 2007).

Womack, Sr. John, "What is the Call to Ministry?" D.Min. diss., Gordon-Conwell Theological Seminary, 2001.

Woods, Ellen. "Higher Calling." *Military Officer,* September 2006: 103.

Yanez, David. *My Military Life and the Power of God.* Houston: RevMedia, 2006.

OTHER SOURCES CONSULTED

Adams, David L. *The Anonymous God*. Saint Louis: Concordia, 2004.

Alford, Deann. "Faith, Fear, War, Peace." *Christianity Today* (December 2004), http://www.ctlibrary.com/17054 (accessed October 14, 2008).

Air Force Personnel Center, "Service Demographics Offer Snapshot of Force." (April 9, 07), http://ask.afpc.randolph.af.mil/pubaffairs/release/2007/4/demographics.asp (accessed October 25, 2007).

Air Force Policy Directive 52-1. (2 October 2006) "Chaplain Service." http://www.e-publishing.af.mil/pubfiles/af/52/afpd52-1/afpd52-1.pdf (accessed October 25, 2007).

Ayers, Jule. "From the Chaplaincy to the Pastorate." *The Covenant Quarterly*, Vol 5, No. 1 (Fall 1945): 59-64.

Barna, George. *Generation Next*. Ventura, CA: Regal Books, 1995.

Blackaby, Henry and Claude King. *Experiencing God*. Nashville: Broadman and Holman, 1994.

Clapper, Gregory. *Living Your Hearts Desire: God's Call and Your Vocation*. Nashville: Upper Room Books, 2005.

Christopherson, Richard. "Calling and Career in Christian Ministry." *Review of Religious Research*, Vol 35, No 3 (March 1994): 219-237.

Coffey Jr., John. *God is My Pilot*. Nashville: Thomas Nelson, 1968.

Cox, Jr., Harvey, ed. *Military Chaplains: From a Religious Military to a Military Religion*. Nashville: Abingdon Press, 1969.

Cross, Christopher. *Soldiers of God*. Richmond: William Byrd Press, 1945.

Davis, David. "St. John Chrysostom on Ministry, Discernment, and Call." *Theology Today*, Vol 62, No 3 (October 2005): 408-413.

Dickens, Williams. *Answering the Call: The Story of the U.S. Military Chaplaincy from the Revolution through the Civil War*. Dissertation.com, 1999.

Du Bois, Lauriston. *The Chaplains See World Missions*. Kansas City: Nazarene Publishing House, 1946.

Dulles, Avery. *Models of the Church*. exp.ed., New York: Doubleday, 2002.

Drake, Butch. "Excuse Me, But Have You Ever Considered Ministry?" *The Disciple*, Vol 132, (October 1994): 16-17.

Eck, Diana. "What is Pluralism?" http://www.pluralism.org/pluralism/what_is_pluralism.php (accessed October 25, 2007).

Elkins, Dov Peretz. *God's Warriors*. Middle Village: Jonathan David Publishers, 1974.

Farnham, Suzanne and Joseph Gill, et al., *Listening Hearts: Discerning Call in Community*. Harrisburg, PA: Morehouse Publishing, 1991.

Other Sources Consulted

Farnham, Suzanne and Stephanie Hull, et al., *Grounded in God: Listening Hearts Discernment for Group Deliberations*. Harrisburg, PA: Morehouse Publishing, 1996.

Farnham, Suzanne. *Listening Hearts: Manual for Discussion Leaders*. Harrisburg, PA: Morehouse Publishing, 1993.

_____. *Retreat Designs and Meditation Exercises*. Harrisburg, PA: Morehouse Publishing, 1994.

Graves, Joel Curtis. *Leadership Paradigms in Chaplaincy*. Dissertation.com, 2007.

Guffin, Gilbert. *Called of God: The Work of the Ministry*. Westwood, NJ: Fleming H. Revell, 1951.

Guinness, Os. *The Call*. Nashville: W Publishing, 2003.

Leuschner, Martin et al. *Religion in the Ranks*. Cleveland: Roger Williams Press, 1946.

McCasland, David. *Oswald Chambers: Abandoned to God*. Nashville: Thomas Nelson, 1993.

McDowell, Josh. *The Last Christian Generation*. Holiday, FL: Green Tree, 2006.

Morsch, Gary and Dean Nelson. *The Power of Serving Others*. San Francisco: Berrett-Koehler Publishers, 2006.

Olsson, Karl. "Mission of the Chaplain." *The Covenant Quarterly*, Vol 4, No. 1 (Fall 1944): 40-45.

Plummer, David. "Chaplaincy: The Greatest Story Never Told," *The Journal of Pastoral Care* 50 (1996): 1-11.

Turabian, Kate. *A Manual for Writers of Term Papers, Theses, and Dissertations*, 7th ed. Chicago: University of Chicago Press, 2007.

U.S. Army Chaplain Recruiting Pamphlet, "Answering the Call." U.S. Government Printing Office (July 2006).

Veith, Jr., Gene Edward. *God at Work*. Wheaton: Crossway, 2002.

Warkentin, Marjorie. *Ordination: A Biblical-Historical View*. Grand Rapids: Eerdmans Publishing, 1982.

Watson, David. "Professing the Call to Serve." *Quarterly Review*, (Spring 1982): 27-42.

Weston, Logan. *The Fightin' Preacher*. Alexander: Mountain Church, 2001.

ABOUT THE AUTHOR

Chaplain, Lt Col Brian Bohlman has served in the U.S. Armed Forces since 1992 and is currently assigned as the Wing Chaplain at the 169th Fighter Wing, McEntire Joint National Guard Base. He has served in support of the following military operations: Bright Star, Northern Edge, Sea Signal, Noble Eagle, Enduring Freedom, and Iraqi Freedom. In 2013 he received the Samuel Stone Award and was named the Air National Guard Chaplain of the Year.

His civilian Chaplaincy experience includes ministry in a hospital trauma center, life flight helicopter rescue, and correctional facilities. He has also provided volunteer Chaplain services to police and fire departments, as well as civilian businesses. He is a graduate of Liberty University, Columbia International University, and Erskine Theological Seminary.

In addition to his military service, he serves part time as a behavioral health Chaplain and teaches Chaplaincy courses at Columbia International University and Liberty University Baptist Theological Seminary. He is the author of numerous articles about professional Chaplaincy and the books, *So Help Me God: A Reflection on the Military Oath* and *For God and Country: Considering the Call to Military Chaplaincy*.

In 2002, his family founded Operation Thank You.org as a 501(c)(3) non-profit organization to inspire faith, promote patriotism, and support our troops by providing inspirational and patriotic resources and programs for service members, veterans, wounded warriors, and military families. In 2007 Operation Thank You was recognized for excellence at a White House ceremony.

For God and Country: Considering the Call to Military Chaplaincy

Brian is an active member of numerous organizations including America Supports You, Officers' Christian Fellowship, Military Chaplains Association of the USA, Association of Professional Chaplains, National Guard Association, American Legion, Military Officers Association of America, and the Celebrate Freedom Foundation. He and his wife and daughter reside in South Carolina.

He is a frequent guest speaker on radio and television programs as well as in churches, community and veteran organizations. He has over 23 years of experience in the areas of post-traumatic growth, resiliency, spiritual wellness, suicide prevention, grief and loss, post-deployment reintegration, and marriage enrichment.

Brian welcomes the opportunity to speak at your next gathering or special event. He is an inspirational and sought after speaker for retreats, workshops, conferences, prayer breakfasts, graduations, enlistment and commissioning ceremonies, worship services, and other church, civic or patriotic events.

If he can be of service to you or your organization, please contact him through www.OperationThankYou.org or www.ChaplainResourceCenter.com.

To order any of his books in paperback or e-book, visit Amazon.com/Author/BrianBohlman

CPSIA information can be obtained
at www.ICGtesting.com
Printed in the USA
LVHW081554150319
610804LV00017B/584/P